CITIES OF SIGNS

minding the media

CRITICAL ISSUES FOR LEARNING AND TEACHING

Shirley R. Steinberg and Pepi Leistyna
General Editors

Vol. 5

The Minding the Media series is part of both
the Peter Lang Education list and the Media and Communication list.
Every volume is peer reviewed and meets
the highest quality standards for content and production.

PETER LANG
New York • Washington, D.C./Baltimore • Bern
Frankfurt • Berlin • Brussels • Vienna • Oxford

Andrew T. Hickey

CITIES OF SIGNS
learning the logic of urban spaces

PETER LANG
New York • Washington, D.C./Baltimore • Bern
Frankfurt • Berlin • Brussels • Vienna • Oxford

Library of Congress Cataloging-in-Publication Data

Hickey, Andrew T.
Cities of signs: learning the logic of urban spaces / Andrew T. Hickey.
p. cm. — (Minding the media: critical issues for learning and teaching; v. 5)
Includes bibliographical references and index.
1. Sociology, Urban. 2. Urban anthropology. 3. Cities and towns—Growth.
4. Signs and symbols. I. Title.
HT151.H46   307.76—dc23   2011046856
ISBN 978-1-4331-1120-4 (hardcover)
ISBN 978-1-4331-1119-8 (paperback)
ISBN 978-1-4539-0541-8 (e-book)
ISSN 2151-2949

Bibliographic information published by **Die Deutsche Nationalbibliothek**
Die Deutsche Nationalbibliothek lists this publication in the "Deutsche
Nationalbibliografie"; detailed bibliographic data is available
on the Internet at http://dnb.d-nb.de/.

Cover photo and concept by Andrew T. Hickey

© 2012 Peter Lang Publishing, Inc., New York
29 Broadway, 18th floor, New York, NY 10006
www.peterlang.com

To Shelly, my love and motivation.

For my boys, who I hope will continue to find this world a source of wonder and creativity. It is for you that I undertake this work in order to understand those places we inhabit that little better.

To Shirley and the memory of Joe, whose work as academics, activists and engaged human beings demonstrates that the things we do as scholars must always result in something positive.

In the postmodern context, individuals are rendered more vulnerable than ever to the power of the image.

—Joe L. Kincheloe, The Sign of the Burger

Contents

Acknowledgments

A number of people have been crucial to the production of this book. Firstly, my colleague Jon Austin graciously gave his time to read and comment on those various drafts that culminated in what is before you. He was also a guiding influence as I first set out on my explorations of urban space and public pedagogy several years ago. His considered responses as a critical friend, fellow traveller and expert field researcher have made this book a far stronger one than it otherwise would have been.

To my partner, Shelly, and my boys, Dylan and Zac, whose interest, support and patience while I was preparing this book cannot go without mention. Your love and support are cherished and it is for you that I do the work that I do.

The publisher of this book, *Peter Lang Publishing*, must also be recognized for their willingness (and the risk taken) to publish a work written by an Australian academic on evidence drawn from fieldwork undertaken in the global 'south'. A friend and colleague of mine at another Australian university noted how difficult it is to find publishers willing to take on books without a 'northern', mass market appeal; '*the potential market is too small*' is a familiar response. In particular, Chris Myers and Sophie Appel in the New York office provided sound advice and support from the very beginning and made the production of this book an entirely enjoyable process. So to these ends, I thank *Peter Lang Publishing* for taking me on.

Finally, I must acknowledge the influence that Shirley Steinberg and Joe Kincheloe have had on my thinking and my work as an academic. Both Shirley and Joe have taught me that one must remain humble whilst undertaking work of significance and meaningfulness, and it is in their image that I have attempted to do just this. I hope that this book goes someway to living up to these ideals. To Shirley especially, who (with Pepi Leistyna) secured the publication of the series within which this book resides, I am indebted to you.

Introduction

The Logic of the Now

The public is completely uninterested in knowing
whether the contest is rigged or not, and rightly so; it
abandons itself to the primary virtue of the spectacle,
which is to abolish all motives and all consequences:
what matters is not what it thinks but what it sees.

—Roland Barthes, *Mythologies*

Nothing is as it seems in the urban landscapes of our contemporary world.
Towering images of airbrushed promise rise from every corner. Elusive
détournéments find overlaid (but usually temporary) refuge on authorised
surfaces. Prescriptions on how to travel, eat, live and have fun confront at the
slightest opportunity, whilst directives on where to walk, talk and *be* hint at
the underlying sanctions present in those spaces we encounter. This is the
contemporary city; a space of signs and symbolism at once rich and
prescriptive, ideal and imagined. A space of visually broadcast
pronouncements, transmitted from the fronts of billboards, traffic signs,
itinerant graffiti and similar other public communiqué, all made meaningful
in acts of interpretation engaged in by those who read and consume the
messages sent.

The mediated messages of signs—of *who* we are, who we *might* be—
find purpose in the urban streetscape. The promises they contain read
according to who it is we want to be, who it is we can be. Meanings
produced as we negotiate our urban habitats conflate with larger cultural
assumptions. The signscape reflects back to us ourselves as it reveals the
logics of our culture. In the communicative interplay that occurs between us,
the sign and those shadier intentions that exist behind them, we see the rules
of the game. Here is where the cultural logic of a space forms and makes
itself apparent. Here is where those deep desires of our collective union find
expression and interpretation. Here is where we learn about ourselves and the
conditions by which we must operate.

The variously pragmatic or directive intent of the sign does not matter so
much as its interpreted purpose. It is how the sign comes to gain meaning as

an interlocutor of deeper cultural intentions that is important. The sign provides the context upon which the interplay of social communication occurs. As a site that exposes the deepest values of our societies (and one in which we are inculcated as readers whether we realise it or not) the sign exerts an intent and purpose that goes beyond any direct, immediately recognizable 'message' alone. A traffic sign does more than simply direct traffic flows. An advertising billboard does more than simply market a product. An act of graffiti does more than simply détourné an authorised surface. These signs also point to deeper cultural logics. They say something of the very parameters by which a space and its peoples are ordered and function.

Signs do this through the everyday mediation of meanings. As ubiquitous elements of contemporary cities, they stand as fundamental and 'ordinary' markers of urban landscapes. The very *everyday-ness* they carry brings them into unquestioned contact with their consumers; that is, any street-going viewer who happens to cross them. We might find ourselves variously entertained or outraged by the messages they contain, but rarely question the existence of the sign itself. As core components of the mass-communication apparatus of our global world, there is little to be considered *extraordinary* in the presence of a sign. It is as much a part of urban streetscape as the street itself, and from this basis at least, is a largely accepted aspect of the contemporary city.[1]

But this ordinariness shouldn't be confused as incapacity. As much as it might be that the cities of our world are shaped around the road-ways and transportation networks of our oil-powered industrialism, it is via signage that these spaces come to be understood and convey meaning. This is a visual-symbolic era, with signs authorising the practices of urban space according to their visual form. Signs configure the symbolic ordering of the urban space as a *cultured* space; ordering its interpretive limits and framing the gaze of the interpreting viewer. The sign is a site upon which something might be learned through the visual encounter it provokes. They are active enculturators, speaking of the ways of culture, the limits of acceptability and the nature and sensibilities of a space. For this reason, they must be noticed—this is where culture manifests, is made meaningful and finds transmission.

It doesn't matter that the promises made by signage are often inflated,

---

[1] This normality extends in some instances to the urban space being defined precisely by its signs; to the point that in some cases, such as Times Square or Las Vegas, the very identity of the urban space is *the* sign. Signs in these cases become a little extraordinary because they are indeed so ordinary—but it is the *amount*, and not the signs themselves, that makes these urban spaces that little bit extraordinary.

hyper-real and fantastic. This is not the point. We as viewers, in the sort of way that Barthes (1972) notes, accept these contrivances (and perhaps come to expect them). This is the nature of the interplay; the fantastical hyper-reality of the sign doesn't need to translate into reality. All the sign need do is point to our hopes and desires, fears and anguishes, to do its job. Signs speak symbolically of what is *underneath*; they point to the cultural *id* that we know is there, but which we symbolically obfuscate. Ignoring the sign isn't an option; the logic of the sign has been established already in the consciousness of the viewer. We know what the imagery says long before the sign is even crafted, before it casts its view over the world. It has to make sense; its meanings are already formed in the cultural logic that powers the sign's creation. The sign is merely the manifestation of something culturally much deeper.

Even the most benign of signs hints at the ways we understand our social world and move to structure it (and ourselves). Signs carry the purpose of those individuals or groups that put them in place, and must be viewed as core elements of the communication apparatus of urban space. Of course, different signs will carry different purposes, and will mean different things to different people, but within that range of interpretive possibilities, and from the multitude of purposes the *sign-as-communication artifact* might carry, something can be understood about the nature of the space in which the sign makes its appearance. Signs provide a tangible form upon which the deep workings of culture might be explored.

It is from this basis that this book draws its motivation.

Chapter 1

Signs and Cities: The Contemporary Cityscape and the Nature of Symbolism

> The construction of consumer subjectivity and desire must
> move beyond some simple, direct appeal to the individual; it
> must rearrange larger social structures and cultural forms.
>
> —Joe L. Kincheloe, *The Sign of the Burger*

The Surface of Things

A quick look down any urban streetscape will reveal an array of signs in one
form or other. Directional and 'traffic' signs stand as a feature of most
traffic-oriented urban spaces, whilst billboards and similar advertisements
provide an insight into the sorts of consumption habits that are practiced in
our economically globalized world (Figure 1). Graffiti and other
détournéments (such as illicitly pasted posters and stencils (Figure 2) might
also be noticed, as well as the very architecture by which the streetscape is
arranged (Figure 3). The uses to which urban space is put (this too should be
considered a 'sign'), and the way physical space configures action by people[1]
(Figure 4) are also important, and will suggest something of the social
practices and conventions local to that space. Whether operating explicitly
(such as traffic signs) or in more symbolically implicit ways (such as the
usage of a streetscape), all of these things stand as a *sign* of a space and
provide symbolic reference to the underlying *logic* maintained within it. It is
through signs, and what they mean to those who encounter them, that
something about the distinctiveness and identity of a space might be learned.

---

[1] The operations of the decreasingly seen traffic warden provide an obvious example of the
human being as sign. But so too should any individual who exists, as they are, where they are
in the streetscape. The very act of being where one is contributes to the meaning of the space.
These operations of being contain symbolic complexity and richness, just as a billboard, work
of graffiti or traffic sign might also.

Figure 1: A typical streetscape. Photo: Andrew Hickey.

Figure 2: Illicitly pasted posters in one downtown space. Photo: Andrew Hickey.

Figure 3: Détournément: The reworking of space as signified via signage. Photo: Andrew Hickey.

Figure 4: The typical shapes and forms that signify a typical city. Photo: Andrew Hickey.

From this, we might say that the logics of culture find expression in signs. Signs convey cultural meaning; that is, they indicate what is central to a culture and the manner by which understandings of the world come to be framed and understood. As mediators of the cultural logic, signs present a surface upon which negotiations between the underlying symbolic codes of cultural meaning and the physicality of space (because all cultures are 'located') might be interpreted. This is important, as it is with signs that physically situated interlocution of deep-held cultural logics find expression, ready for consumption by those who read them. The way signs come to mean and what they represent provide insight into the way culture is produced and framed, as it accords to the *situatedness* of its location.

Herein lies the central intent of signs; they interpret those underlying cultural logics of a space, whilst simultaneously articulating assertions of what that space *is*. Signs stand as manifestations of the symbolic codes that order a space, but similarly act as messengers for what it might be. Conveyed by signs are suggestions and directives, hints and pronouncements that order the space and maintain its logics for all who read its messages. This very much makes them important sites of investigation for any analysis of culture and its constituent practices.

A Case in Point

One such example of this signed insight into the cultural logic of a space exists not far from my home city, in a rural valley district located between two large urban centers. Signage (Figure 5) on the side of the highway that cuts through the district suggests that strong religious affiliations are held— *Christian* as it happens, in what might be called an 'evangelical' flavor.

Amongst a group of signs that variously denote the presence of churches in the area and encourage passing motorists to engage with this brand of religion stand a series of three signs that broach the controversial topic of abortion and 'right to life' (Figures 6, 7 and 8).

Figure 5: Proclamation by roadside. Photo: Andrew Hickey.

Figure 6: A roadside billboard containing a culturally rich message. Photo: Andrew Hickey.

On the surface of things—or at least, on the surface of these billboards— it might be accepted that this district has a clear sense of itself, is unified by religion and maintains an image of self powerful enough to activate public roadside pronouncements on issues as complex and controversial as abortion. From these signs and the intent of their message, an indication of this district's philosophical and moral logic might be gathered—*here is a community that presents a strong affiliation to a particular brand of Christianity and subsequently feels it necessary to comment publicly, via the mobilization of signage, on an issue it feels to be significant.* These are the sorts of assumptions that might be gained about this space and its inhabitants, as suggested by its signs.

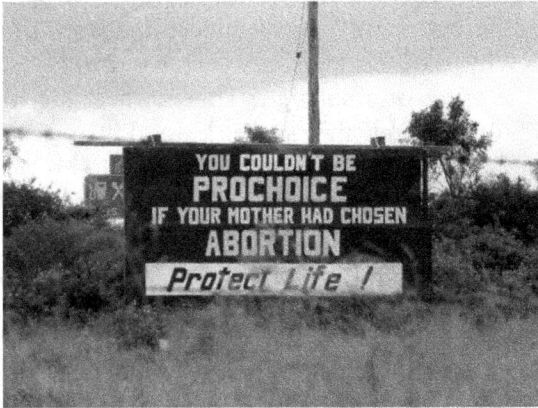

Figure 7: An accompanying billboard. Photo: Andrew Hickey.

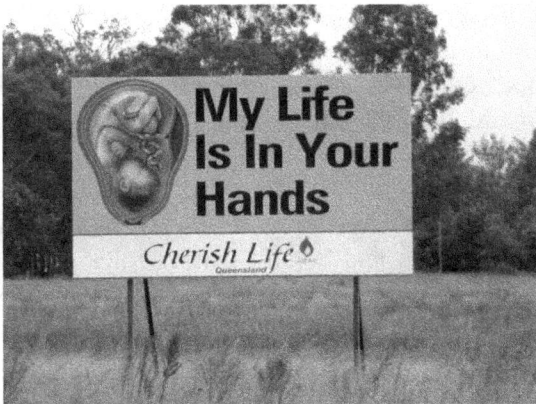

Figure 8: The most recent addition to the roadside pronouncement. Photo: Andrew Hickey.

But the signs themselves didn't tell everything there is to know about this community. I realised this as I happened to be traveling past one day and noticed that one of the signs had been vandalized, with the principal text of the original sign spray-painted over in black, and new text added; *'its your choice'.* All of a sudden my initial views of this community were overthrown and the emergence of an alternative world-view voiced. Here stood an active response to the sign (and its underlying logic), albeit one that was unauthorised and illegally overwritten (this was by definition 'graffiti' and 'vandalism'). What this now suggested was that an alternative viewpoint was present within this community; that a monological framing of this issue no longer maintained primacy. A series of questions immediately struck me; was this détournément the work of an outsider, a passer-by from some other community with different views? Was it indeed the work of someone within the community? Why did this person/s feel so strongly as to risk being caught in order to alter the original sign? This is where the sign stopped short in telling me something about this space. I was left guessing as to *exactly* what was going on.

While it was clear to me that signs such as the *'right to life'* signs could convey certain ideas about the cultural logic of the community within which they stood, the story was far from complete. A closer, *ethnographic* look would be required in accompaniment with an analysis of the signs themselves. While the signs provided clues—as outwardly physical expressions of ideas, attitudes and beliefs—an analysis of those operations of power and agency that authorised the hosting of these signs and their messages would also be required.

Signs as Documents

Of course, presenting a certain view of things is what signs do. They do indeed tell us about ourselves and what we consider significant enough in culture to say something about. This might not always be blatant and active; some signs might carry far more coded messages, or capture the logic of cultural assumptions that function inconspicuously as taken-for-granted aspects of 'ordinary' life-ways and life-styles (assumptions concerning leisure, consumption habits and certain gender roles stand as examples of things that are often presented and accepted according to wider cultural assumptions of what is *normal*). Even the most seemingly inconsequential of signs—those accepted without any fuss or controversy—have something to say beyond what their explicit message might initially suggest.

It occurs that to know something about the operation of signs as cultural artifacts—their intent, the manner by which they are interpreted and how they come to be understood—a larger inquiry than that provided by the reading of signs alone is needed. To understand the manner by which signage is produced and consumed requires an investigation of the workings of both signs as artifacts of culture *and* the role they play in those spaces in which they operate. The purposes to which they are put and the ways that they are 'read' and considered is a vital aspect of this process of *reading* signs.

It is how signs as documents provide a sense of what exists within the *boundary*[2] of social understanding that is at stake here. Although we see reflected back from the front of signs deep-held assumptions of the world and the logics by which we understand it, to have an impact and in order to hold their end of the bargain, signs must make 'sense' according to the logics of their settings. So that we might read and gain some idea of what has been intended in their message, the sign must connect to what it is we expect to find signaled by them. In the acts of communication they deploy, signs must retain connection with the sensibilities of the culture in which they operate; the sign is as much a representative of our deep cultural logics as it is a reinforcer of these. The specifics in the detail of the message presented by the sign might well be new and prompt a reconfiguration of our understandings (of all manner of phenomena encountered in culture), but in conveying this message, it must still work within the bounds of the cultural logics of that space.

An example of how the overreach of cultural sensibilities might be provoked within signage occurred on a set of billboards that advertised (of all things) a specific brand of shoe in Australia through 2002. A sort of national debate (which involved federal ministers of government) ensued when two billboards advertising a line of men's shoes included seductively posing young women with a double-entendre-ridden slogan that suggested that excesses of heterosexual pleasure would befall any man who purchased a pair. This clearly wasn't an expression of *reality* (the shoes weren't that good), but the production of a certain type of desire (an age-old advertising mechanism) that sparked public outcry due to the extent that women's (and for that matter, men's) identities were being presented in a contrived and outwardly sexualized way. This wasn't what people wanted to (or indeed *should*) see, argued the billboards' critics, and the adverts were eventually withdrawn and the contract between the shoe manufacturer and billboard advertising agency ceased. In this case, the logic by which these signs presented and situated their view of the world extended beyond what the community expected of them; signs must operate within the boundaries of our understanding and the sensibilities of culture in order to work. If they extend the cultural logic too far, they cease to mean. What can be said then, is that signs, if they function within the boundary of cultural sensibility, provide insight into the logic of culture due to their very acceptability and the display of ideals they capture in their messages.

Reading Signs

To suggest that signs are 'read', and that meaning comes from those acts of

---

[2]   As Anthony Cohen (2004) would see it.

interpretation engaged in as a part of this practice (a *cultural literacy* of sorts), isn't itself a new proposition. Any sign producer will note that the provocation to produce a sign is to have others read it. But how signs capture, in a deep epistemological sense, the nature of our culture and then work to reinforce its central logics is significant and the focus of scrutiny in this book. I wish to explore the *public pedagogical* intent of signs and signage, specifically as it occurs in urban space (a site in which signage is at its most prolific and exposed). How we *learn* from signs and what this says about who we are, both as individuals and members of cultures in this visually saturated twenty-first century, will form the core intent of the inquiry contained here.

In this book, I draw attention to urban spaces specifically, but in doing so, do not intend to suggest that signs are significant to urban spaces alone (signs clearly also work in regional and non-urban spaces). But due to the sheer intensity and frequency with which we see signs in urban spaces, it follows that for any inquiry interested in understanding how signs work, exploring sites where signs are both prolific and blatant in their operation will provide fertile locations of study. Equally, this of course isn't to suggest that all urban spaces operate in the same way; clearly, they do not. But it is within urban space *generally*, as it is configured and shaped in most parts of the increasingly globalised and inter-connected world, that one is likely to see, amongst the visual culture contained within urban space, the presence and operation of signs. Signs work from a primarily visual medium. Cities are visual spaces. It makes sense to investigate signs in these highly visual settings.

In doing this, I apply a tripartite theoretical basis for establishing signage as a point of sociological analysis. Firstly, it is of signs themselves that I am principally concerned. Whether in the form of simple street signs offering directions, the re-touched promises of billboard advertising or the vandalizing détournéments of street-art, through to the formations of urban space via architectural arrangement and the social practices engaged in by people inhabiting these spaces, signs pervade urban space and provide a tangible text upon which the logics of both cities and ourselves are written. Signs, and the communication interplay they are there to fulfill, are both manifestations of those logics we configure our culture against, and expressions of culture in production. It is this insight into the workings of culture, via the symbolic manifestations that signs provide, that I am principally interested with here.

Secondly, the space within which these cultural artifacts reside is as important to the meanings made of them as the signs themselves. Without a context, signs are emptied of their purpose and meaning; it follows that knowing something of the spaces in which they exist is essential if any reasonable attempt to understand the significance of signs is to proceed. This includes, of course, the operations and practices engaged in by those people present in these spaces, and the multitude of ways in which they react to the signs they confront.

The third concern drawn upon in this book builds on both of these theoretical bases and focuses attention to the ways that we, as human beings, relate to these signs. While the production of signs and the intentions behind their meanings are a significant concern, so too is the way that signs are consumed and read. More specifically, focus will be given to the public pedagogical intent of signs. What is it that signs intend and how is it that they come to be read? There is a phenomenological concern suggested here, as it taps into the bases of understanding and the hermeneutics engaged in by those who read the signed urban landscape.

Taken together, these three focus areas situate the theoretical orientation taken in this book. I will suggest that urban space is, at least in part, identifiable due to its signage, and that signage itself is authorised and validated by its placement in urban space. It is within this mix, and the communication channels that signs generate (signs require readers, readers require signs), that pedagogical intentions exist. We inhabitants of urban space not only *read* but also *learn* our way through the signscapes of urban space. The significance here is not simply to do with the manner by which signs clutter public spaces, or even in the extent of the ideas they present, but (more precisely) in how signs position our understandings of the world and each other. The experiences from a selection of case examples drawn on in the later chapters of this book will work to demonstrate the educative nature of urban space, and the operations signs play as key elements of the urban communication apparatus.

Empirical Groundings

This book charts explorations of public signage drawn from fieldwork undertaken in Australia. In the explorations presented later of *Greater Springfield*—that master-planned edge city located in south-east Queensland, Australia, that with much fanfare through the late 1990s and 2000s created suburban spaces including *Springfield Lakes* and *Brookwater*—I chart an analysis of the way in which signs *create* spaces (and, more intrinsically the identities of those who live there). These case locations offered key examples of the way contemporary (sub)urban developments go about transforming space.

These locations also have the distinction of being locations far less exposed to the academic gaze of 'northern' (Connell 2007) urban theory, and provided me with a view of urbanity and city life perhaps different to those from the 'great' cities of the ethnographic imagination—New York, Chicago, Los Angeles, London and Paris, principally. Although I am not at all suggesting that work in these classical locations has 'been done', or indeed should finish, it is the case that the locations drawn on in this book haven't been theorized anywhere near as heavily as those staple spaces of urban sociology, and as such, may prove to be refreshing sites of sociological inquiry.

What is contained here is the culmination of experiences in these urban spaces, and my own theorizations and thinking on how we, as human beings existing in a world of global flows and large-scale urbanization, come to mark and make sense of our urban habitats. Concerns for signs and their existence might seem somewhat like a sociology of desperation (a project to explore something, *anything* connected with human existence), but it is to what signs refer, and how they mediate a pedagogical influence, that is important. This is a project that seeks to uncover the very workings of culture—these signs situate a point of rupturing from which underlying cultural logics break through and manifest as *artifacts* (for sociological analysis) on the physical surface of culture.

As part of the built environment, signs exist in two senses; i. as physical artifacts, designed with purposeful intent and aesthetic characteristics, but also ii. as points of symbolic transmission, of ideals and values, practices and mores. As I referred to above, the significance of signs isn't simply in the existence of the signs themselves—it is not solely in how these artifacts of culture beam back to us certain messages. The concerns presented in this book are for how we, as citizens of the most highly urbanized epoch of human existence, come to relate to these spaces and the educative effects of signage within this dynamic. In short, this is a book about the functioning of culture, and the way that signs provide a physical *guidebook for living* by tapping into and making apparent the core logic of culture.

The Limits of Theory

The ideas presented in this book do not claim to function as grand theorizations. The case examples, instances and situations reported will be presented according to the contexts in which those examples, instances and situations made sense to me; the unique contexts from which they emerged during my time in them as ethnographer. This sort of theorization is grounded in the specific experience derived from those sites *imprecisely* reported on. I say 'imprecisely' because it was via an interpretive process, driven by my observations and experiences (as epistemologically grounded in my own way of viewing the world) that the selection, analysis and translation processes typical of sociological/ethnographic inquiry came to be presented here for you to read and make some sense of. While I sincerely hope that the experiences reported here may be of use to sociological theorizations of space more generally, I will not attempt to claim that the lessons drawn from the case sites examined should in any way be understood as standing for *all* situations. With this I take Denzin and Lincoln's suggestion that:

> Qualitative research is a situated activity that locates the observer in the world. It consists of a set of interpretive, material practices that make the world visible. These practices transform the world. They turn the world into a series of representations... (2005:3)

To the reader of this book I say this: read this work as a portrait of specific case sites produced according to the confines of specific contextual conditions that are now abstracted within this book by an ethnographer who shaped his understandings of these spaces against his own epistemological predilections. As a sociologist and ethnographer, I will stand by the rigor with which the fieldwork underpinning the evidence-set presented here draws its impetus (and the analysis of evidence provided later should demonstrate a strength of methodological design and process). But I will also stress that the way I came to view and frame what was seen and what was interrogated 'in the field' speaks both to the uniqueness of the case sites as cultured locations and the bounds of my own interpretive gaze. As such, I suggest that the reader do with these findings as she or he sees fit. There is nothing universal contained here, but simply a report on various case sites as they appeared to me at the time that I was a part of them. Again, this should by no means diminish the significance of this work; I hope that it is still entirely valuable in what it has to say about the way urban space functions. But in doing so, it acknowledges that ethnographies derived from partial visions of case sites developed by ethnographers who 'write' the world as much as they report on it will never speak *Truth*. I discuss these concerns further in *Chapter 2*.

Theoretical Groundings

Just as the methodological practices applied here are framed around certain agreed upon 'ethnographic' processes for reading the world sociologically, so too are the theoretical foundations drawn on to contextualize the ideas captured in this book. In order to lay bare some of the ideas and traditions drawn on in the later chapters, a survey of the key literature that informs this book follows.

Urban Space: The City and the Sociological Imagination

Although more comprehensive and authoritative surveys of the development of urban sociology can be found elsewhere (Gottdiener and Hutchison 2006; Flanagan 2001; Borer 2006), a few points detailing the way *The City* has been conceptualised and theorized in sociology should be stated. Interest in both the idea of the city and the spaces that constitute its geography have a history in sociology almost as long as sociology itself. The first generation of sociologists, including such heavyweights in the Western intellectual tradition as Durkheim, Weber and Marx, to varying degrees each drew on the idea of the city by situating it as the location in which that great preoccupation for the early sociologists—*modernity*—was most visible. For these theorists, the mid-nineteenth-century city represented a site in which the bonds and life-ways of large groups of individuals (and more specifically, where the operations of such things as bureaucracies and industrialization took place) might suitably point to the orientation and rise of modern ways-of-life. The way people functioned according to the scale and forms of organization prescribed by cities hence formed the backdrop to grand theories on humanity and the nature of modern life; including the locations in which Durkheim's 'solidarities' might be seen to occur, or the tensions between Toennies's 'Gemeinschaft' and 'Gesselschaft', for example. These studies situated the city as a key site of new forms of human habitation, heralded by modernity and the industrialization that was taking place in those European cities of which they wrote. The city was a site of complexity and modern life practices that stood in contrast to older, agrarian, non-urban life-ways witnessed in the not too distant past.

Moving beyond the concerns for the city as a site of macro-level workings of modernity and industrialization, more specific attention was afforded the city by Georg Simmel. Beyond being simply the location within which new forms of human group behaviour might be explored, Simmel saw the city as a phenomenon in itself, and set about charting a more genuinely 'urban' sociology through an urbanism interested in individual human responses to city life. Simmel's classic work 'The Metropolis and Mental Life' (1997a) set about explaining the psycho-social conditions of the city, and introduced influential ideas to explain the urban experience—the city dweller's 'blasé' attitude stands as a key example. For Simmel, human beings were capable of processing only so much sensory input, whilst the city on the other hand was saturated with potentially overwhelming sensory stimulants. To cope, the urbanite must learn to filter out 'the loud and impinging but also irrelevant' (Gottdiener and Hutchison 2006:47) aspects of city life by focusing on only that which is *required* and *needed*. Simmel notes:

> The psychological basis of the metropolitan type of individuality consists in the intensification of nervous stimulation which results from the swift and uninterrupted change of outer and inner stimuli. Man [*sic*] is a differentiating creature. His mind is stimulated by the difference between a momentary impression and the one which preceded it. Lasting impressions, impressions which only differ slightly from one another, impressions which take a regular and habitual course and show regular and habitual contrasts—**all these use up, so to speak, less consciousness than does the rapid crowding of changing images, the sharp discontinuity in the grasp of a single glance, and the unexpectedness of onrushing impressions. These are the psychological conditions which the metropolis creates.** (1997a:175 *emphasis added*)

Unable to cope with the totality of the sensorium of city life, the city dweller, unlike his rural cousin, must pick and choose according to what is needed and required from the complex of inputs available in the city. The city dweller only has so much cognitive space to fill, so must choose according to a blasé attitude what is let-in and what is let-pass by the 'conscious layers of the psyche' (175).   This was an important development in early urban sociology. Apart from attempting to make some sense of the human response to the city, it also provides an indication as to what a profound effect industrialization and modernity were having in the cities of the 1800s—we get a sense in Simmel's work that the modern industrial city was an overwhelming leviathan that directly impinged on the psycho-social stability of its inhabitants. The city was bigger than humanity itself.

Simmel also positioned the urbanite on an evolutionary scale of human development. When founding member of the Chicago School Robert Park announced that the city 'is the natural habitat of the civilized man [*sic*]' (1967:3), he drew upon Simmel's suggestions that the pace and flurry of urban life gave rise to a sophistication of being—a refinement of humanity and intellect. This sentiment is captured when he notes:

> Thus the metropolitan type of man [*sic*]—which, of course, exist in a thousand individual variants—develops an organ protecting him against the threatening currents and discrepancies of his external environment which would uproot him. He reacts with his head instead of his heart. In this an increased awareness assumes the psychic prerogative. Metropolitan life, thus, underlies a heightened awareness and a predominance of intelligence in metropolitan man. (Simmel 1997a:176)

City life, as it was for Simmel, not only kept one on one's toes, but also refined the senses as it sharpened the wit.

Although Simmel's ideas carried favor for the next half-century and represented (along with the social theory of Emile Durkheim, Max Weber and Ferdinand Toennies) some of the most dynamic and important work in the (then) fledgling discipline of sociology, it was in the highly urbanized, completely modern and heavily industrialized new world of the United States that the next development in urban sociology emerged. Whereas the first generation of European sociologists situated the city as a site from which questions of social organization, industrialization and modernity might be examined, it was with the Chicago School and the ethnographic explorations by its founding sociologists during the first half of the twentieth century that a sense of the intricacies of life within the city were made. By getting out and getting 'the seat of the pants dirty' as Robert Park (1927) famously implored his students to do, the Chicago School sociologists identified the role of close observation for understanding patterns of urban life. Drawing on the theoretical insights of the first generation of sociologists (particularly Simmel) and the idea that 'every portion of space possesses a kind of uniqueness, for which there is almost no analogy' (Simmel 1997b:138), the uniqueness and vagaries of living within urban space became the focus for Chicago urban sociology.

Applying a *human ecology* approach, Park suggested that city life represented a microcosm within which human behavior could be understood according to *biotic* and *cultural* factors. Within this ecological model, the biotic referred to factors such as competition and survival, whilst the cultural contained the processes of symbolic exchange that occurred within these spaces. Mobilizing this approach, Park set about exploring the city—down to the way that people came to live and conduct themselves within it—according to the ecological conditions it presented. Spaces within the city were presented as microcosmic elements of the larger urban ecology, and it is from this work that we see development in the conceptualisation of the city as an entity made up of inter-connected parts.

This *contextualized situatedness*, as I call it, of urban investigation was a defining feature of the Chicago School approach, and is what draws together a large and disparate body of work under the title *Chicago School Sociology*. The approach gave prominence not only to the city-space as an organic entity in its own right, but also to the primacy of those local practices that occurred within it. It was an interest in what occurred within the unique 'local' settings of the city that features as a common thread in studies such as Thrasher's (1927) *The Gang*, Wirth's (1928) *The Ghetto*, Zorbaugh's (1929) *The Gold Coast and the Slum*, Frazier's (1932) *The Negro Family in Chicago* and

Hayner's (1936) *Hotel Life*. These definitive Chicago School studies continue to be cited as seminal works in urban sociology.

Whilst the modus operandi and design of these studies were familiar (Gottdiener and Hutchison note that '*this marvellous output was produced with a similar stamp*' (2006:56), they showed that the intra-urban complex was something worthy of investigation. It wasn't so much that the city was influenced and shaped by outside forces (such as the macro-economic and industrial societal formation concerns of the first generation sociologists), but that the city framed its own ecologies, and hence contained its own patterns and logics. Here was a paradigm for exploring the city that saw the city in and of itself, according to the uniqueness of its ecology. As Wohl and Strauss note, 'even the oldest resident, and the best informed citizen, can scarcely hope to know even a fair sized city in all its rich and subtle detail' (1958:524). These familiar places turned out not to be so familiar at all; the complexity and scale (both symbolic and physical) of the city became the terrain for significant social research.

Following not long after the golden era of the Chicago School (an era that extended into the 1940s) came the development of the urban *political-economy approach* of the late 1960s. Drawing on theoretical foundations provided by Marx and Weber, the political economy approach focused on the city in terms of its evolutionary supplanting of agrarian society through capitalist, industrial-economic growth. Here the modern city represented the location—a physical manifestation—of processes of capitalist economic development. Hence, its theorists argued, the contemporary city took on a form unique to capitalist development and became a site in which the methods of exchange, operations of power, structural shape and societal organization core to capitalist economics might be witnessed.

Frederick Engels's (1887/2009) studies of the industrial cities of 1800s England, written a century before political-economy urban sociology formed, stand as a key point of origin for many of the later works in this area. Engels demonstrated how the dynamic of capitalist expansion in the formation of industrial cities (particularly his study of Manchester) established a concentration of both capital investment and labor within the same spatial zones. But it was the manner in which wealth could coexist with extreme poverty and social dysfunction that caused him to question the human costs of this expansion. Beyond the 'extended conditions' of the industrial city, Engels drew attention to the division of class by location within the intra-urban space, and the manner with which social practices were maintained and reproduced across generations (themes that sociologists including Paul Willis (1977) and Pierre Bourdieu (1987) would engage a century later). The city for Engels was a place of vast division and concentration at once; a location established to service the needs of industrial capitalism via the close proximity of money and labor, and through the spatial practices of class segregation and enclave neighbourhoods.

It was from this basis that Henri Lefebvre's work emerges. Grounded heavily in a Marxist reading of capitalist economics and via an interest in the mechanisms by which appropriations of space occur, Lefebvre draws attention to the way space is named and used. Core to this are ideas that have been influential in sociologies of space since; in particular his idea of *détournément* (borrowed from the *Situationists*), the *circuits of capital* that mobilize possibilities for the way space is constructed and used, and *abstract* and *social space* that signify different perspectives for considering the role of space. These provided Lefebvre with the foundations to explore the construction, manifestations and uses of urban space, with his interpretations of détournément particularly distinguishing his sociology. As he notes:

> An existing space may outlive its original purpose and the raison d'etre which determines its forms, functions, and structures; it may thus in a sense become vacant, and susceptible of being diverted, reappropriated and put to a use quite different from its initial one. (1991:167)

It is the idea of appropriation that holds significance for Lefebvre. Appropriated spaces open opportunities for the re-appraisal of the production and utilisation of space, and hence, open opportunities for resistance and demonstrations of agency:

> The diversion and reappropriation of space are of great significance, for they teach us much about the production of new spaces. During a period as difficult as the present one is for a (capitalist) mode of production which is threatened with extinction yet struggling to win a new lease on life (through reproduction of the means of production), it may even be that such techniques of diversion have greater import than attempts at creation (production). Be that as it may, one upshot of such tactics is that groups take up residence in spaces whose pre-existing form, having been designed for some other purpose, is inappropriate to the needs of their would be communal life. (1991:167–8)

The value of Lefebvre's ideas lay in his identification of the way space is 'produced' and invested with meaning. He offers an opportunity to conceptualise space outside of (what he calls) its 'geometrical meaning' (1991:1), and opens the possibility of critiquing the function of space and the implications of power relationships in those 'spatial practices' (1991:8) that occur within any space.

It is from the work of a group of social geographers loosely banded under the term *postmodern geography* that some of the more dynamic recent theoretical developments in urban sociology reside. Engaging postmodernity's multiplicities that 'allow new possibilities to emerge that were hidden behind traditional ways of explaining the world' (Malpas 2001: 10), postmodern geography marks a significant break with earlier models for understanding urban (as well as sub-urban and inter-urban) forms. In these new terms, considerations of urban space are reconfigured so that:

> ...the sprawling metropolis has become much less monocentric, less focused on a singular downtown; and is no longer as easily describable in terms of distinctively urban, suburban and non-urban ways of life. (Minca 2001:43)

Following these sentiments, Edward Soja notes:

> In my view, there has been a significant transition, if not transformation, taking place in what we familiarly describe as the modern metropolis, as well as in the ways we understand, experience, and study cities. (2000:xii)

Drawing heavily on his experiences in Los Angeles and the megacities of the United States, Soja highlights that with the evolution of post-industrial and increasingly global society, the corollary change and transformation of cities has resulted in shifted conceptualisations of what cities *are* and how they function. He suggests that these new urban spaces represent a 'postmetropolis', a new formation of urban space that carries with it reconfigured ideas about the built environment and the interactions humans might have. In a similar manner to the way political-economy urban sociology viewed the city as a manifestation of capitalist economics, the city for Soja stands as an expression of 'the globalization discourse...an encompassing paradigm for all studies of the contemporary' (41). As he continues:

> The more specific globalizations of capital, labor, and culture have had the cumulative effect of producing the most heterogeneous cities in history, and this extraordinary diversity (often too simply labeled multiculturalism) has become the hallmark of postmodern urbanism. Such heterogeneity is expressed in architecture and the design of the built environment, in the organization of urban labor markets, in the formation of local community and identity, in urban politics and the planning process, and in almost every facet of everyday life.... (41)

The postmetropolis is thus an expression of the globalized world order of the late twentieth century.

Other recent work in urban sociology focuses variously on the 'experience' of city life (Merry 1981; Colombijn and Erdentug 2002; Parker

2004; Bridge 2005), the role of the city as a spatio-political location (Karp, Stone and Yoels 1991; Holston 1999; Davis 2000; Soja 2000; Tajbakhsh 2001; Hall and Miles 2003), the globalized nature of contemporary cities (Light 1983; Hamel, Lustiger-Thaler and Mayer 2000; Clark 2003) and the design and function of urban space (Merry 1981; Brower 1996; Rodruigez 1999). As Soja (2000) notes, this literature represents a shift in thinking about cities that '[p]erhaps more than ever before...is consciously aware of ourselves as intrinsically spatial beings' (6) and that '...for the most part even the field of urban studies has been underspatialised until recently' (7). Drawing on the stock of ideas and theory preceding it, current urban sociology is giving significant attention to the spatial practices and experience of urban (and sub-urban) life as lived by its inhabitants.

Methodologically, Michael Borer's (2006) articulations of the *urban culturalist perspective* that seek to explore 'the lived culture of cities and not merely their economic or political structures and demographic profiles' (174), and Gottdiener and Hutchison's (2006) *socio-spatial approach* both draw into question the experience of the city and the production of meanings engaged in by its inhabitants. Similarly (and somewhat reminiscent of Baudellaire's flâneur), the ethnographic work on the experience of *walking* in the city as charted by Demerath and Levinger (2003), as well as Mommaas's (2004) discussion on the politics of 'cultural clusters' in the post-industrial city and Frers and Meier's (2007) exploration of the manner by which a city's visuality is ordered and produced each represent this concern for the lived-experience of the city and its spatiality. Common to these works is a focus on those practices of meaning production engaged in by inhabitants of urban spaces.

Urban (and) Community

A key point of focus for this book (and ongoing attention in urban sociology generally) is the relationship between community and the city. The complexity of urban space and the transformations in human inter-relationships these spaces prompt caused early theorists such as Durkheim and Toennies to suggest that *community*, as it was understood in the non-urban, agrarian settings they explored, would be impossible to maintain within the city. This is a theme that carries on to the present.

In 2005 the Australian financial services group *Australian Unity* in conjunction with Deakin University's *Centre for Quality of Life* released the *Wellbeing Index: Report 12.1 Special Report on City and Country Living*. The report sought to identify '...how satisfied Australians are with their lives and life in Australia' by investigating '...satisfaction with economic, environmental and social conditions in Australia, as well as giving ongoing insights into our perceptions of individual wellbeing' (Australian Unity 2007:1). A large portion of this report examined the relationship of place to personal wellbeing and emphasized the role physical spaces play in the creation of feelings of happiness. Various urban and non-urban places were examined according to the feelings of connectedness individuals had within them, with *Chapter 4: Community* dealing specifically with the function of community in the maintenance of personal wellbeing. Within this, community was understood as both a 'structure of feeling' and a physical location. It was something that came to represent a point of interpersonal connectedness where satisfaction and wellbeing were intimately associated with physical spatiality and locatedness—a theme similarly picked up by Bauman (2001) when he suggests that '[i]t feels good...it is good to have a community, to be in a community' (1).

One of the outcomes of the report suggested that:

> In terms of satisfaction with safety and community connection, the values for people living in cities is lower than for people living in all other locations. It is evident that high density living produces less interpersonal connection and a diminished sense of safety. (Cummins, Davern, Okerstrom, Lo and Eckersley 2005: 2)

The widely publicized results of this report identified that city life doesn't yield connections to community, interpersonal bonds and senses of wellbeing that otherwise occur in less urbanized locations (Cummins, Davern, Okerstrom, Lo and Eckersley 2005). Whilst cities may provide the potential for access to services and complex social networks, they do (at least in the contemporary Australian context as the report notes) promote a sense of disconnection and impersonal ties between individuals.

These results are by no means unique to Australia, with recent studies from the United Kingdom and United States identifying similar outcomes.[3] Feelings of dissatisfaction with city life correlate with popular but largely romanticised ideas of urban decay and declining personal safety, with these feelings further represented by trends such as the 'sea change'—that escape from the urban maze in search of richer, therapeutic and more interpersonal associations supposedly found in archetypally imagined coastal and rural communities. Cities, in these manifestations of the public imagination, operate as locations of alienation and entities that are perceived as '...either

---

[3] See particularly Amanda Crook's article from the *Manchester Evening News* (13th March 2005), Nilary Duncanson's article from the *Daily Record* (28th April 2006) and Glasser and Shapiro's (2003) survey of urban living in the United States, as well as Lebo's (2007) accounts of neighbourhood ties within cities.

dangerous and alien to the men and women who try to live there, or lacking in substance, paradoxical, and unbelievable' (Timms and Kelly 1985:152). Addington (2002) continues these themes by noting that he '...felt it somewhat paradoxical that one can get a feeling of isolation even when surrounded by people' (3).

The city becomes an 'unreal' location; one in which 'bad' things happen. Popcorn (1992) suggests that due to fears held about urban spaces, the nature of contemporary consumer lifestyles and increasing individualism, the phenomenon of 'cocooning' features as an important aspect of collective, urban living. For Popcorn, cocooning says much about the nature of urban space and the way that individuals conceptualise themselves and others within an environment that contains perceived dangers on every corner:

> The daily news is worse today than a year ago. Headlines scream out tales of horror and violence. Home remains our only safe haven, our sane retreat from all this chaos. City streets are dim and dangerous, very 'Clockwork Orange'— with wilding gangs of bandits and hordes of homeless and the mentally deranged. (Popcorn 1992:201)

Mike Davis (2000) has theorized what he notes as 'an ecology of fear' operating in the sorts of locations Caldeira (2005) terms the 'fortified enclaves' of the post-metropolitan city; a fear marked by security obsession and materializing in the form of fortified neighbourhoods, gated communities and privatized residential authorities. This joins with Soja's (2000) idea of the 'carceral city' in which 'post metropolitan modes of social and spatial regulation' mark a new 'regime' of urbanization (44). This is a setting ripe for Zygmunt Bauman's condition of 'mixophobia':

> 'Mixophobia' is a highly predictable and widespread reaction to the mind boggling, spine-chilling and nerve-breaking variety of human types and lifestyles that meet and rub elbows and shoulders in the streets of contemporary cities not only in the officially proclaimed (and for that reason avoided) 'rough districts' or 'mean streets', but in their 'ordinary' (read: unprotected by 'interdictory spaces') living areas. (2007:86)

Connecting with Richard Sennett's (1996) idea of the 'community of similarity', Bauman (2007) notes that *'mixophobia manifests itself in the drive towards islands of similarity and sameness amidst a sea of variety and difference'* (87).

Urban space, according to these visions, isn't something to be engaged. Rather, it is something to be mistrusted, avoided and as much as possible barricaded out. The city is filled with Simmel's (1950) *strangers*, all perceived as doing strange and untrustable things. The underlying theme in these views of cities and city life relates to the inability of community—as a necessary expression of human group interaction—to function in urban spaces. Whilst cities are spaces of dense population and 'busy' individualism, at least in terms of the *Gesselschaft*-like nature of '...our rapidly privatized and individualized, fast globalizing world' that Bauman (2001:15) notes, communities are thought to operate as entities of a 'slower' *Gemeinschaft* of human interpersonal connection. This divide between the impersonality of the city and the close bonds of community is a feature theme in prominent sociologies of city and community, and provides a dualism from which assumptions about human group organization find articulation. Cities as built environments may well be entirely possible without a sense of community, but the belonging, interpersonal connections and sense of value provided by community promote a viability of rich human interaction that cities are (according to the literature at least) in seeming need of. The blasé city dweller simply cannot afford, through fears for personal safety or the over-stimulation of sensory input, to engage too closey with the city for fear that all sorts of *bad* things might happen.

But whether or not cities represent the 'perfect form of human organization' as Park (1967) boldly declared, or are fundamentally dangerous and isolating locations, it must be pointed out that the theme of dysfunction isn't new—as Borer (2006) notes, ideas of dysfunction and alienation have been key aspects in sociological writings of cities since the beginning (177). But yet, people continue to find cities worth living in, and as statistical trends show, the bulk of us now live in urban environments.[4] Whether good or bad, conducive or not to human existence, the city is and will remain a fundamental marker of the human spatial experience. Borer's (2006) point that the 'study of urban cultures is an important and worthwhile task' (173–4) holds true on this count at the very least. It follows that the way the city is thought of, used, constructed and appropriated must also be understood if any sense of what the city *is* might be gained.

Ideas of the City from Outside of the Metropole

In her groundbreaking analysis of disciplinary sociology, Raewyn Connell (2007) explores the politics and cultured nature of knowledge production present in social theory and in doing so identifies a split between 'northern' knowledge, constructed in the global 'metropole', and that of the antipodean 'southern' periphery. As she notes in the introduction to *Southern Theory*:

---

[4] As detailed by a United Nations report (2009), by 2030 the majority of the world's populations will reside in cities.

> ...social science is, at best, ambiguously democratic. Its dominant genres picture the world as it is seen by men, by capitalists, by the educated and affluent. Most importantly, they picture the world as seen from the rich capital-exporting countries of Europe and North America—the global metropole. To ground knowledge of society in other experiences remains a fragile project. (2007:vii)

The problem is that the knowledge created from such a perspective, when presented as generalizable, forgets the experience of the bulk of the world's populations; populations for whom the metropole isn't home. As Connell continues:

> In this light, the making of sociology takes on a new significance. The places where the discipline was created were the urban and cultural centers of the major imperial powers at the high tide of modern imperialism. They were the 'metropole', in the useful French term, to a larger colonial world. The intellectuals who created sociology were very much aware of this...This fact is crucial in understanding the content and method of sociology, as well as the discipline's wider cultural significance. (2007: 9)

The 'making' of urban sociology, and the locations it studied, was no different. As with much of the knowledge that is generated from the metropole, urban sociology has similarly prefigured the experiences of urban life from the centers of the (post)industrialized Western world. The consequences of the generation of such knowledge are, as Connell notes, seen 'in four characteristic textual moves: the claim of universality; reading from the centre; gestures of exclusion; and grand erasure' (44). By situating the concerns of urban sociological theory on experiences drawn from those well-worn sites of inquiry (the London, Paris, New York, Chicago, Los Angeles case sites so often figured) and then proceeding with an assumption that the experiences derived from these locations will speak for the experiences of *all* locations, urban sociology has developed a specific flavor; one of the Western, industrialized and post-industrialized metropolis.

But as Roy and Al Sayyad cogently note:

> Despite the origins of this pre-existing discourse, the phenomenal growth of cities around the Third World in the last four decades indicates that the urban future does not lie in Chicago or L.A., and that it will not be shaped according to the schools of thought named after them. Rather, the future lies in cities like Cairo, Rio de Janeiro, Istanbul, and Bombay, and can best be investigated by looking at them. One important and common characteristic of these places is that older models of urbanism are being replaced by 'new' forms of urban informality that challenge the relevance of previous thinking about 'blasé' urbanites. (2004:9)

Roy and Al Sayyad locate their analysis in the 'informal' urban experience—
that experience of urban space that has been referred to broadly as 'a
temporary manifestation of underdevelopment characterized by survival
activities of the urban poor' (Roy and Al Sayyad 2004:11). Work in 'urban
informality' has centered on the experiences of urban space in locations away
from the metropole—in the megalopolises of Latin America, Africa and
South Asia. The realities of 'extra legal housing and unregistered economic
activities' that account for 'up to 90 per cent of the new housing stock' and
'more than half of the adult population's… employment' (Tranberg Hansen
and Vaa 2004: 7) in these locations point to the vestiges and legacies of
colonialism now manifest in globalized economic regimes. Asef Bayat
(1997) similarly notes that the existence and location within the economic
complex of the informal urban space situates the 'urban informal' within a
system that both marginalizes and exploits whilst retaining as necessary in
the operations of the urban economy this subject position. This is where
urban sociology must now turn—to the experiences of the bulk of the
world's populations who live in urban settings uniquely different from those
of the metropole.

This conceptualisation and reporting of the experience of the informal
urban space marks a fundamentally different approach to the ecological
culturalism of the Chicago School, class divisions of political-economy and
spatialized practices of postmodern geography. From analyses of informal
urbanism, a stark and direct accounting of the urban experience from the
position of the world's *Others* emerges, and with it, a new suite of theoretical
bases that question the politico-economic operations of the metropole when
explaining and making sense of the city. As Roy and Al Sayyad note, 'what
we are talking about are not only different geographies of informality but
also different geographies of knowledge' (2004: 4).

In a similar manner, work on exploring the experiences of women and
views of the city from indigenous perspectives has also prompted a renewal
in understanding the city. O'Connor's explorations of Southeast Asian
urbanism challenges dichotomies of urban/rural by situating the Asian
experience as 'relations of parts' between urban and rural societal structures:

> Southeast Asia's cities have always brought diverse peoples and societies
> together. Urbanism is neither the sum of this diversity nor its common
> denominator but a society of societies, a culture of cultures. (1995:36)

It isn't that a fundamental dichotomy between antagonistic mechanical and
organic solidarities (as Durkheim would see them) is in operation, or that
structures of Gesselschaft and Gemeinschaft (in Toennies's sense) are

dialectically opposed in this new conceptualisation, but that the workings of urban space are understood as being contingent upon the operation of intrinsically inter-connected rural spaces. This conceptualisation of the city speaks of relations of parts to a broader whole; parts that are not, in and of themselves, discrete societal structures.

A similar theme also emerges in Graham and Peters's (2002) and Peters's (1998, 2001) exploration of the experience of first nations women in the city. By situating the city as a site of gendered, racialized and sexualized practices, and drawing on critiques of the historical legacies of colonialism and racial marginalization, Peters poses an 'alternative geography' for situating the urban experience from both a first nation and female perspective. In a similar way to Hosagrahar's (2005) survey of colonial modernity in India, this approach draws attention to the way that space is mediated according to certain identity characteristics, and calls for the deployment of alternative approaches for understanding the experience of urban space as it responds to its situatedness and contextualization.

Appardurai (1996) makes the point that 'modernity is decisively at large, irregularly self conscious, and unevenly experienced' (3), and in the case of the colonial urban experience, conflates the idea of urban development and progress (as marked initially by industrialization, and more recently the post-industrial, information societal transformation of the global metropole) in antithesis to indigenous life-ways found in the antipodean south. As Hosagrahar explains:

> Appropriating history and historiography, Europe constructed itself as the prototypical 'modern' subject. To be 'modern' was the prerogative of European rulers who claimed the right to define its meaning and assert its forms. The definition was based on difference: to be 'modern' was to be not 'traditional'... This fundamental opposition has been the premise of both scholarship and professional intervention in city planning and architecture. (2005:1)

It is clear that the explanations of urban life and urbanism presented by theorists of the metropole don't quite tell the full story. As the work just noted demonstrates, the experience in peripheral locations (focused specifically on identity characteristics and spatial practices that haven't been the focus of the metropole's gaze) provides a set of alternative readings and conceptualisations of the city that might more fully explain the experience of the city in this increasingly urbanized world.

Core Ideas for Conceptualising the City and This Book

Whilst a number of core ideas and explanatory concepts drawn from the discussion above will be applied in this book, two underlying themes will re-emerge regularly. Firstly, and in presenting the experience of *Greater Springfield* in the later sections, I will make a connection between the urban experience and community. As I noted above, for more than a few sociologists and theorists of urban life, community is viewed as being either in serious need of attention and reclamation, or indeed is extinct. I look at community according to the way that Anthony Cohen (2004) saw it working in the villages of Scotland—according to the operation of a symbolic logic that orders and defines the manifestation of culture. It is via the limits of this symbolic logic—the *boundary* as Cohen called it—that a sense of what the community *is* might be gathered. This boundary speaks to the identity of the community and the deep epistemological bases upon which this identity rests.

As Cohen notes, the 'boundary' exists as that point of symbolic exchange that refers to:

> ...an entity, a reality, invested with all the sentiment attached to kinship, friendship, neighboring, rivalry, familiarity, jealousy, as they inform the social processes of everyday life...[it] **is more than oratorical abstraction: it hinges crucially on consciousness**. (2004:13 *emphasis added*)

This is foundational to the idea of community presented here. It is from the *intent* of the boundary that a sense of a community can be gathered, and it is via the operations of the boundary as they manifest in culture that attention will be focused in the explorations presented later.

From this basis, a second theme core to this book emerges; *public pedagogies*. I will argue, from the experiences I had in the case sites reported later, that community functions from both physical and symbolic bases and exerts an educative influence in relaying and affirming cultural logics. As Thrasher (1927) famously noted (albeit somewhat out of context here), 'the street educates with fatal precision' (476); indeed it does, if the examples detailed later are any indication. In particular, it is via signs, and the role they play in the communication apparatus of the contemporary city, that pedagogical intentions will be uncovered and scrutinized. Culture bubbles up from the boundary and presents itself in the workings of culture and its physical forms. It is via signs as one specific but highly intentioned manifestation of the cultural logic that attention will be given in this book.

Signs seek to tell us something of the societies in which they are placed, and hence carry with them intent to instruct. This happens in a variety of ways. In a late-capitalist context, for instance, we might see signage, whether it be 'official' or not, connected to the concerns of global capitalism and subsequently the manufacturing of desire via the mobilization of markets ('advertising', in other words). As one form of signage in this context, most billboards are largely about *selling*.[5] This is symptomatic of the logics underpinning global capital writ-local according to the specific market demands targeted in the locale of the sign. What can be said here is that the sign both encapsulates the logic of those cultural contexts from which it makes 'sense' and is located, and contributes something into the public dialogue (regardless of how one-sided and incomplete that dialogue happens to be).

This of course isn't to suggest that those signs with clear commercial and consumptive motivations are the only ones to worry about. Even the most ordinary and ubiquitous of traffic signs, for example, will tell something of the order by which a society functions. On a very superficial level, the presence of a traffic sign, for instance, automatically suggests something of the presence of 'traffic' and hence the operation of road networks. More structurally, concerns about global warming and other issues caused by the operation of those vehicles the sign mediates might be arrived at. However superficial this basic analysis might be, the point here is that signs (as the name would suggest) function as *signifiers* pointing to deeper meaning and exegesis beyond the surface-level pronouncements they make.

This is a cultural concern. Culture, as that thing that binds us together, operates from a necessarily symbolic basis in that it exists outside of each of us, but is core to our being. It is culture that provides the symbolic logic by which we understand *how things are and how things come to be*. While we might see expressions of culture presented in physical 'artifacts' (such as the signs explored in this book), it is to what these artifacts refer that is important. As humans, we are deeply symbolic and understand the abstracted connections between signifier and referent to the point that codes of logic related to the very act of living, being, representing oneself and understanding one's 'situation' in the world are encoded in the format of our culture. In this global-economic age, with its vast divisions in the distribution of wealth and differential opportunities for the expression of agency in the politico-economic complex, the manifestation of culture operates according to more than the material conditions we experience; it is symbolically coded. Hence, I will suggest that what is *seen* in culture—the way it is formed and framed—manifests in terms of symbolic codes translated into the physical spaces of our world. As part of the production of culture, human beings produce cultural artifacts that contain the intent of their desires, and present this to the world via such publicly pedagogical mechanisms as signs.

---

[5]   Except for the few that could be considered to have genuinely philanthropic, government-motivated public awareness or resistive détournément motivations.

These are the core themes from which this book will present its case. In doing so, it will present an argument for the conceptualisation of culture as the dynamic interplay of individuals with varying levels of interpretive agency and a symbolically coded communication apparatus that manifests physically in such spaces as *the* city. From the mobilization of this production of culture come public pedagogical interests—proclamations of what culture is, how one is to live life within it and how the physical landscape shall be configured to support these logics. Following a discussion on the method by which I argue that urban space might be explored in the next chapter, I turn in *Chapters 3* and *4* to a survey of selected case sites to support the assertions presented here.

Chapter 2

Looking Again: Reviewing the City with Fresh Eyes

> Community as a phenomenon of culture...is meaningfully
> constructed by people through their symbolic prowess and
> resources.
>
> —Anthony Cohen, *The Symbolic Construction of Community*

*How should urban space be considered? Is it enough to only look at the form
and shape of the built environment when making assumptions about how the
space 'works', or should consideration of the ways that people use and make
sense of it also enter the equation? At what point does the symbolic
manifestation of culture give way to the simply practical, utilitarian form of a
specific building or streetscape, if indeed it ever does? When thinking about
space in this way, is it even wise to install a dualism by which the physical
form of space might be seen as something separate from—perhaps even
antagonistic to—the symbolic, or is this an indication of a failure in the way
a space has been conceptualised? These are questions that analyses of the
cultured nature of space must encounter.*

Chapter 1 provided an indication of the orientation for viewing and
understanding urban space as it applies in this book, but to build on this and
provide some further indication of the ways that those urban spaces explored
in the following chapters came to be understood (both by the inhabitants of
those spaces and by me as ethnographer), this chapter will detail the
approach and method through which these analyses were cast. In doing this, I
do not wish to spend inordinate time retracing a particular style of urban
ethnography, nor provide detailed exposition of specific urban sociological
field methods (apart from briefly noting how a field method for encountering
the city might commence). These concerns are taken up elsewhere (see
particularly Borer 2006; Gottdeiner and Hutchison 2006). The focus of this
chapter lies in the contemplation of those epistemological concerns that
arbitrate urban sociological research—considerations related to how

understandings of urban space are generated.

To begin, those urban spaces explored in the chapters that follow were seen to operate according to two aspects of culture that are intimately inter-connected and inseparable; the *physical* and the *symbolic*. Consideration of both aspects was fundamental for any interpretation of how these spaces functioned. It was not solely in the shape and design, nor the symbolic ordering alone that full indications of how these spaces were considered and 'lived' emerged. The symbolic generation of meanings contained within a space will be influenced by the way that space takes shape, but similarly, the physical shape of the space and the way it manifests as an entity will speak of underlying cultural logics that inform its creation. Cities, like any location invested with human meaning, will always operate according to these two aspects; as humans we build our physical environments against those symbolic ideals we invest in culture, but similarly, the shape of culture is always necessarily framed by what the physical form of the world allows.

As highly organized formulations of space, cities maintain a physicality that is clearly apparent in their built environments. This aspect of a city predisposes the experiences able to be had within it; experiences had according to how the shape and configuration of urban space mediate human activity.[1] This is the first concern that must be encountered by any analysis of how a people go about living their lives within the city as space—one interested in the sheer physicality of the space in question. How we come to *be* (that is, how we come to be situated existentially according to those cognitive processes of meaning making human beings engage when 'making sense' of where they are) in urban space is in part reflected in how the city is shaped.

It is this consideration for the roles of physicality in the ways individuals come to use and conduct their lives in space that apply in this book. But more specifically, it is the way that signs (as one specific and prominent set of urban artifacts) mediate the city that is given particular attention. Signs are *tricky* cultural artifacts. As clearly visible elements of the landscape, they appear not only as an expression of the physicality of urban space but also (importantly) as a tangible surface upon which the underlying symbolic order of a space materializes and gains form. At the same time that signs maintain a physical presence (as indicated by their very existence in the streetscapes of the city) they also do something more; they enact a symbolic transference of

---

[1]   For example, Demerath and Levinger (2003) suggest that 'walking' in the city provides a unique connection to the built environment of the city; one unable to be engaged in as fully from the position of motorist. From these positions—positions structurally mediated by the physical form of the city—two very different experiences are generated.

meaning drawn from the cultural logic of the site. Hence, signs operate not only from the first aspect of the city, its physicality, but also from the second, its symbolic ordering. They exist at the intersection of the physical and the symbolic, and for this reason are significant artifacts for the consideration of how urban space is experienced.

Of course, signs are not alone in this mediation of the symbolic and physical—just as much might be learned about the cultural logic of a particular urban space from the way residents build neighbourhoods (such as those detailed by Graham and Peters 2002 and Frers and Meier 2007) and relate to the ways that urban planning practices configure the spaces they live within (see for example Demerath and Levinger 2003), or how resistant social practices expose the deeper logics by which urban space is programmed (such as those detailed by David 2007). But it is from the sign, as one common, visible, and physical artifact of urban space, that opportunities to explore the cultural logics core to a site present themselves in a (simultaneously) symbolically *rich* and physically situated manner.

But this isn't all signs do. Beyond providing an interface upon which the physical and symbolic aspects of culture manifest, signs also position those spaces within which they reside as sites of learning. Because they exist as physical artifacts situated *in* space, and exert intent in framing the underlying cultural logics of a site, they operate as portals of conceptual meaning transference and cultural production. Signs point towards a symbolic mode of meaning construction designed to be read; that is what they do. They exist to inform and convey meaning, with this feature of signs holding true for the largest billboard to the most indiscriminate act of graffiti. Framed by the cultural logic inherent within a space, and mediating the messages they carry according to this, signs act as interlocutors in the transference of meaning, inculcating viewers who decode the messages they present in the process.

We are left with two areas of consideration when undertaking an exploration of urban space and its signage. It is not enough to launch a sociological exploration of a space through signage alone. Some understanding of how these signs are read and consumed must also form part of the analysis. Whilst the first operations of such an inquiry might lay in the workings of the signage itself (what the signs *say*, how they are situated and for whom they are intended), the second must seek some understanding of how people go about engaging with the ideals this signage presents; are these ideals accepted or rejected, do they transfer smoothly and does the limitless interpretive agency of those individuals who will read the sign become configured in certain ways? It is here that the pedagogical implications of signs—that is, how they exert an educative influence—must be excavated. This is the concern of this book.

Epistemological Locations

It follows that the methods by which we look at and explore urban space will influence the ways we come to understand it. This is the case not only for formal, intentioned sociological investigations of a space (framed as they are by academically determined and established methods of inquiry), but also informally in the ways that 'ordinary' residents and users of urban space come to know and interpret their surroundings. It is the *idea* of the space that is at stake here, and how that idea is framed that exposes the epistemological processes of meaning making engaged in by those making the meaning. Dean MacCannell highlights this point in a key example of how meanings are framed:

> I know a lady who lived at the foot of a famous mountain in Northern California, who saw it everyday for three years, and who was perfectly aware of the name of the mountain and its fame, but who did not know that 'her' mountain was 'that' mountain. (1999:137)

We develop our experiences from both the physicality and the underlying symbolism contained within a space *as it appears to us and according to how we frame our understandings of it.*

Formal sociological accounts of the world operate in the same way when framing their understandings. Even when couched in established methods of inquiry and with assumptions and 'findings' derived from sources of evidence that can be shown to have been rigorously acquired, what is left is still just an account of the world that is framed in particular ways, according to specific epistemological markers. The implications for this must be acknowledged; sociological interpretations of the world 'do not produce timeless truths' (Denzin and Lincoln 2005:16). As sociologists, we frame and configure our understandings in certain ways, according to what is seen and how this empirical knowledge base is negotiated to form understandings of those spaces in which we do our work. What is reported here is no different.

What Should Be Learned from Sociological Accounts of a Site?

What might the purpose of sociological inquiry be? The benefit of a (methodologically and epistemologically) well-performed sociological inquiry must lie in the depth of its analysis and its *multivocality*. While sociological accounts of the world should sit 'in the middle' (Saukko 2005: 345) amongst other accounts produced by people variously engaged in the living of lives, sociological analysis has the imperative to seek 'deep' accounts of a site through the soliciting of multiple points of view across sustained periods of time. We undertake sociological research in order to seek engagement with individuals involved in the day-to-day business of living lives; to do justice to this and to have our reportings from these sites mean anything, they must provide a view that is, firstly, as faithful as possible to the views of those individuals with whom we conduct sociological research (our informants), and secondly, rich with evidentiary sources that cut across experience and positionality to provide as complete an image as possible of the site being investigated. If any understandings of the sites we enter are to carry weight, those 'larger' understandings we seek of them must be underpinned by rigorously performed engagement, whilst also acknowledging that any account produced will always be partial and incomplete, generated as these sites appeared at the time.

The central understanding that must come from any sociological account of spaces in which human beings live lives is that there will never be any *Truth* to be uncovered, but that what is available is a sociologically mediated view of a site as it appeared to its inhabitants and the ethnographer at the time it was produced. If we accept that 'all such representations of an urban milieu...are inherently unstable' (Wohl and Strauss 1958:532), then there is no holy-grail of exegesis to be found in a key informant or exalted source of evidence; these too will be partial:

> Even the oldest resident, and the best-informed citizen can scarcely hope to know even a fair sized city in all its rich and subtle detail. (Wohl and Strauss 1958:524)

What sociological accounts must always attempt to capture is *depth*. This is 'thick description' as Clifford Geertz (1973) would see it. It is from this sort of account of a site that a dialogue on a set of phenomena, noticed as being interesting and worthy of further investigation, might be opened and an account of the site developed. There is no *Truth* being spoken, but a provocation for considering the world as it was understood from the perspective of those people drawn into the account at that time. The reportings contained in this book operate in this way. Whilst I will vouch for the rigor by which the analyses provided in this book were produced, what is contained here are reportings of specific case sites *as they came to be understood by me* during sustained conversation with inhabitants of these spaces during the time I was there. They are, therefore, partial.

Methods of Inquiry

Michael Borer makes a case for an urban sociology that does two things:

> Persons' experiences in and of the city are not just a matter of meanings and representations, but of the full consequences of those meanings and representations as well. A full sociological account of cities would need to examine both the representations and symbols of the city and the conditions under which those representations and symbols emerge, solidify, and/or mutate. (2006:179)

He argues that any account of urban space must investigate both 'what culture does to people as a set of imposing ideas that define social order' and 'how culture is passed down and used by individuals as a repertoire of practices'. This is a foundational idea in Borer's case for an *urban culturalist* approach in sociology; culture becomes the interface between human beings and the *place* that the physical forms of the city become when invested with human meaning.

Continuing, he notes:

> ...most of the debates in urban sociology never connect the two faces of culture nor do they recognize that culture is both 'out there' and 'in us'. Perhaps it is best to say that culture is 'through us'. (181)

Significantly, Borer's ideas show that space (in this case, urban space) is never expressed by its physicality alone. Spaces, once invested with meanings shaped by cultural logics, become *places* known and understood via the sense-making processes of human cognition. These are sites of culture, shaped by what the space provides and how it is that people come to use it and think about it.

This book applies this view of urban space. In the case studies detailed in the following chapters, it is from the interplay between those 'structural' aspects of the urban landscape and people's agentic making of meaning within these locations that emerge ideas of what the culture of the urban space *is*. This is a situated concern—one that sees culture as existing within and between spaces and people. We make meaning of our worlds, but simultaneously construct meanings according to what confronts us. In cities, the form of the built environment shapes our understandings just as we shape cities to reflect our desires. What is needed in sociological accounts of space (such as the one contained here) is a method by which space might be understood according to both its form and the phenomenological processes of meaning making engaged in by its inhabitants. This requires an investigative toolbox of skills that allows for both the semiotic investigation of space, as well as inquiry into people's held beliefs and attitudes. The approach utilised here applies an interpretive sociology that takes on the concerns of a *cultural studies* analysis of culture and cultural artifacts, overlaid with phenomenographic exploration of people's held beliefs, to do just this.

Understanding Culture

Signs are carriers of culture and present back to us affirmations of those deep-held assumptions we adhere to as cultured beings. Signs can indeed sometimes go too far and break out beyond the limits of the cultural 'boundary' (Cohen 2004), but more often than not, they simply sit, going about their business with little fuss, all the while informing us about who we are and how we should go about continuing to be who that is. Via signage, placed within the contextual complex of the city, we learn (at least in part) what culture expects from us. This is a semiotic process, and within this a 'cultural literacy' of sorts is required to make sense of the way that signs carry cultural assumptions and how they do their work in framing urban space.

The analyses of urban space in this book drew on an approach that provided scope to explore the 'shape', 'purposes' and 'meanings' (Williams 1989) of those sites explored in the following chapters. Via all manner of evidentiary input—conversations, semiotic deconstruction of roadside billboards, coffee shop chats, observations at art exhibitions, noticings of illicit graffiti, newspaper readings, perusal of corporate advertisements, recalling of personal experiences, amongst myriad other sources of evidence that provided an insight into what it meant to be *in* these spaces (culture is everywhere after all)—accounts of what these sites and their signs suggested were crafted. In other words, a field-based ethnography formed the basis of the method utilised to read those sites I report on later.

I relied heavily on a photographic record of my time in these sites. These photographs documented those various signs and artifacts that I couldn't collect and take with me. The photographs also gave a visual indication of the ideas circulating in each site, and provided the next best thing to actually having them in front of me. They also feature as a major part of the analyses presented in this book. Two forms of photographic evidence were collected—*artifactual* photographs captured the detail of individual signs and evidence sources, whilst *contextual* photographs, particularly those capturing the location and physical layout of the signage in relation to other signs and landmarks were also taken to provide visual reference for my analyses.

It must be noted that these photographs do not stand as 'truths' in and of themselves; they are not timeless and irrefutable extractions of a *reality* captured. I draw on Douglas Harper's suggestions that:

> While the basis of the image is the reflection of light off surfaces of the world, human choices actually create the photo: framing, the creation of blur, color or

lack there of, depth of focus. Other humanly organized frames—taken for
granted assumptions built into culture—define one aspect or another of these
choices as meaningful (for example, a photograph of a certain gesture is only
meaningful to the culture that defines the gesture). Thus a photograph is a result
of human actions and subjective interpretations; in cultural studies terminology,
photographs are polysemic. (1987: 213)

I actively selected, framed and drew my assumptions from very specific
epistemological and pragmatic positions. Firstly, I had a purpose for which
my research was being conducted—to chart the way signs mediate the
cultural dynamic of urban space. This purpose framed what I chose to
capture photographically from my observations and led me to seek certain
forms of evidence according to the concerns they presented (these
photographs were selective). Secondly, the phenomena being captured
weren't 'static' cultural productions, and altered and changed according to
how they were considered and understood. Culture is dynamic, with my
recording and reporting of the phenomena I noted standing as one snapshot
of these things *as they were, in that space, at that time*. I tried to
contextualize this evidence as much as possible in my field notes and against
those other sources of evidence collected. Hence, my photographic evidence,
like all sources of evidence drawn on in the analyses that follow, was 'read'
and analyzed according to how it was situated within a larger cultural
context. In strict methodological parlance, this is called *triangulation*.

Much the same approach was applied to the field conversations I had
with those research participants I encountered. Although now getting a little
old,[2] James Spradley's notion of 'the ethnographic interview' suitably
defines the approach I apply in my own field practice. As he suggests:

It is best to think of ethnographic interviews as a series of friendly
conversations into which the researcher slowly introduces new elements to
assist informants to respond as informants. (1979: 58-9)

In conjunction with the photographic evidence, conversations with
participants form a core evidence base for this book; it is from these that an
indication emerges of how the urban spaces explored here came be
considered and 'lived'. These conversations also provided a basis from
which my photographic and documentary evidence could be read and

---

[2] A librarian at my university will recoil in horror at this. He personally applies the
assumption that anything beyond five years old is too far out of date to be worthwhile. I,
however, stick to the notion that sometimes *good* knowledge can stand the test of time; my
assertions, of course, being supported by those 'classics' regularly cited in academic works.

assessed. Particularly in those conversations where I asked participants to offer their analyses of my assumptions of their cities, I had a chance to see if my summations of the cultural dynamic carried any weight.

Making Sense of Things: Analysis in Urban Sociological Research

Once an empirical basis had been gathered upon which an understanding of those spaces I explored might be made, it came time to shape these into some form. Again, the processes applied in formal, sociological research have protocols for the interpretation and presentation of knowledge, but ultimately, what is sought is the sort of thing Wohl and Strauss refer to:

> Looking at the city, even if it be with an imaginative stare, is only the beginning of the search for the meaning and quality of urban life. What is seen, literally or in the mind's eye, must be expressed and interpreted. (1958:527)

The process applied for interpreting those evidence sources presented in this book drew on a critical ethnographic approach that was used to uncover the ways that culture was produced and enacted. Critical inquiry into how social power was applied to shape ideas stood as a hallmark feature of the interpretative process. This was expressed according to my own concerns for the way that public pedagogical production of meaning was witnessed in the case sites, and the manner by which residents came to understand *their* city. In essence, the process applied the following questions to those sources of evidence collected during my time in the field:

1. How are persons and locations identified and referred to?
2. What traits, characteristics and qualities identify them?
3. What deeper logics contextualize these traits, characteristics and qualities?
4. What can be said about the culture of the site?

These questions were deployed as analytic prompts in my reading of the documents, images and discussions captured as part of my fieldwork. Together, these questions formed a useful launching point for deconstructing the evidence utilised in this study and provided a consistent point of inquiry that underpinned the interpretations I made.

The Purpose of (This) Sociological Work

All sociologies carry some purpose or focus of investigation, and go about realising this focus through the collection and analysis of phenomena considered important. No single sociological account of a site can be everything to everyone however, and part of this resides in the way that sociologies frame their intentions around a particular 'problem'. Sociological accounts of the world are focused inquiries, set into action according to specific purposes. The inquiries that appear in this book are no different and contain a set of intentions grouped around concerns for the way community functions in contemporary cities and the cultural mechanisms by which ideas about these communities find articulation. These concerns prefigure ideas of *public pedagogies* and the manner by which ideals and modes of living are expressed as part of the cultural logic of the city.

Public pedagogies function as acute mediations of the cultural logic by shaping the way culture is formed. Public pedagogies frame the cultural logic of a site in specific ways and according to certain interests—these aren't neutralized manifestations of a culture emergent as some 'organically' arranged understanding or response to the world. They aren't necessarily democratically mobilized nor do they necessarily represent the interest of the 'whole'. They may be generated from the concerns of corporate interest, or come from the desires of a political regime or the interests of powerful members of a sub-group. Public pedagogies confront the cultural logic in ways that shape it; they carry specific interests and ideals for how the culture of a space *should* be enacted. In short, public pedagogies exert *intent* in shaping the cultural logic in specific ways, according to specific interests.

Henry Giroux (2004) makes the point that in this current age of neo-liberal politics and increasing corporatization of the public sphere, some of the more significant public pedagogical manifestations we see infiltrating the cultural logic derive not from the interests of communities or a democratic public, but from far more privatized quarters. Contained within these infiltrations are desires that often aren't in the public interest (but present as such in order to carry favor and provide a warm and inviting 'corporate face'). They represent the vested concerns of capital accumulation writ-large in terms of ethics of consumption and leisure. As Giroux notes with reference to the ways popular culture—one intense site of operation of public pedagogies—is manufactured in specific ways:

> ...[it is] clear that the production of meaning, social practices, and desires—or what can be called public pedagogy—must be addressed as both an educational issue and a matter of politics and institutional power. (2001:4)

Whether manifesting in children's films (such as the critique of *Disney* productions Giroux highlights), schooling and education, or more generally in community, public pedagogies present as manipulations of the cultural logic; these are not 'organic' or 'natural' negotiations of culture undertaken by 'the public', but signify direct involvement in the shaping of culture (usually) by corporate interest. To counter this, Giroux calls for a cultural politics that unmasks public pedagogies to provoke critical readings of culture and cultural production:

> This suggests a pedagogical approach to popular culture that asks how politics of the popular works to mobilize desires, stimulate imagination, and produce forms of identification that can become objects of dialogue and critical investigation. (2001:110)

In the following section, I detail public pedagogical activity as it relates to the formation of ideals such as 'community' and 'belonging' in a master-planned urban development. A set of ideals associated with these sites operated as signifiers of the public pedagogies present in these communities. These took form in sets of keywords and thematic tropes that tapped into *paleosymbolic*[3] ideals of community and human inter-connectedness, and represented specific assumptions that framed the developers' views of Greater Springfield.

It was from these ideals and the manner by which they were disseminated that a sociological 'in' presented itself. Seeing the sorts of desires presented in the artifacts that these new urban spaces hosted, and the mechanisms by which they were deployed to shape meaning, an exposure of the public pedagogical operations present in Greater Springfield emerged. The methodological implication here sits with the way that examinations of the cultural logic might be conducted so as to expose the operations of those public pedagogies present in a site. The mechanisms by which human beings make sense of the paleosymbolic formation of themes like community and belonging are intrinsically connected to such an analysis. Critical semiotic exploration of this signage and phenomenographic dialogue with residents were the methods applied here to gain these understandings.

What I am suggesting here is the operation of a field-oriented sociology interested in the workings and formations of culture.[4] Signs became that surface upon which public pedagogical intentions became visible and from which competing manipulations of the cultural logic could be understood. A purposeful and deliberately enacted sociology of critique emerges within such an approach. This is an approach that actively seeks out the operations

---

[3] Kincheloe provides a definition of paleosymbols that applies here. He notes that paleosymbols denote those meta-level symbolic icons that 'signify significant human relationships—the love of family and place—and the leisure and security that come with them' for example (Kincheloe 2002:49).

[4] This should not be a startling proposition—it is after all what sociologists attempt to do.

of culture—its central logics and formations—to expose the mechanisms by which it is shaped and mediated. It asks questions of significant actors in the social dynamic and how they enact their agency in shaping the world. It seeks both an 'insider' (*emic*) depth of analysis, while at the same time it attempts an 'outsider' (*etic*) perspective that looks anew at this culture, as if for the first time discovering its ways and flows. Most importantly, this is a sociology that doesn't wish to merely report, but critically uncover *why things are the way they are*.

This was the method deployed in the fieldwork that underpins the accounts provided in the following section. I set out to understand what the cultural logic of those sites being explored *was* according to what the operations of those public pedagogies (carried in its signage) suggested. The purpose was to account for the way these urban spaces came to be understood and lived, by positioning an analysis around the ways that the cultural logic of these sites was mediated by specific public pedagogical operations. I now turn in the following chapters to detail some of those analyses that emerged from this fieldwork.

Chapter 3

What the Signs Said: The Public Pedagogies of Signage

> Hehehehe, People will do anything a sign tells
> them.

—Homer Simpson, *The Simpsons, Episode 312, "Bart of War"*

Case Study: Greater Springfield

This is the story of the development of a suburban community. Taking place not just in terms of its physical-geographic reshaping of a pocket of remnant bushland located in-between two existing cities in south-east Queensland Australia, *community* in Greater Springfield developed also at the level of the symbolic mediation of modes of living. Even if community could be defined in terms of physical locatedness alone (we often talk about going *into* communities, as if these are places to be entered), here was an example where community meant much more. The *idea* of community in this place cut far deeper and corresponded to entire patterns of life, attitudes and collective responses to the world, as much as it did to being somewhere. This is a story of both physicality and the shared meanings and symbolic relationships that occurred in this suburban place.

Greater Springfield is an anomalous place; a literally brand-new edge city. In the early 1990s Maha Sinnathamby[1], a multi millionaire Malaysian with a 'vision' bought the land and set about turning this 'empty land'[2], as he called it, into a twenty first century master-planned community. Built up around several sub-developments (primarily the suburban spaces of *Springfield Lakes* and *Brookwater*, an education precinct known as *Education City*, a proposed health precinct and the commercial hub of the *Orion Shopping and Entertainment Precinct*), the development now stands as

---

[1] Sinnathamby is the chairman of the Springfield Land Corporation and MUR property development group. He is the driving figure behind Greater Springfield and is responsible for its 'vision'.

[2] This 'empty land' had of course a significant indigenous history, and was home to the *Jaggera* peoples, the traditional custodians of the land now called 'Greater Springfield'.

an example of how contemporary urban design principles take account of things like community and the way people interact in urban spaces. But to do this, the development needed a clear conceptualisation of what *community* meant.

Far from being a community that evolved organically and of its own accord through time, Greater Springfield developed a pre-fabricated idea of community that matched the instantaneousness of its physical spaces. Beamed from the fronts of billboards and distributed in glossy brochures and mail-outs to residents and intending residents, very clear ideas about what the place was and how it worked were presented. Contained within the paleosymbols of these signs, insights into the cultural logic of Greater Springfield surfaced. Implicit within these signs were suggestions of lifestyle and collective interaction, as well as more explicit exclamations of concepts such as 'community'. The surfaces upon which these paleosymbols operated presented a guidebook for living that expressed how lifestyle and interaction could be lived in this ultra-contemporary development (indeed, these artifacts extended this logic to suggest how lifestyle *should* be lived within the structural constraints of Greater Springfield's physicality); in short, here were definitions of what this community was and how it should be experienced.

Incorporated within these intentions for what community came to mean in Greater Springfield were ideals that prescribed what sort of person would make Greater Springfield home. While never offering out-right statements on the types of identity characteristics that were *preferred*, Greater Springfield did things far more in keeping with late-capitalism's processes of selection— by connecting firstly with a specific demographic of buyers, and secondly (and more suggestively) by appealing to a specific sense of style and distinction (through the setting of markers of economic and cultural capital that the residents of Greater Springfield needed to meet). There was a definite logic to Greater Springfield built on this definition of both the place and its people.

This production of the ideal of community via an organized mass-communication process departed from the sorts of organic formations that communities of the past once applied. The pre-arranged organization of community groups, the nature of activities available to residents, the formation of sporting and leisure clubs and the arrangement of public space merged with advertised imagery that lifted its cues directly from a cultural logic as pre-fabricated and intended as those buildings and landscapes that styled Greater Springfield. These ideals were initiated and maintained by the developers of the space to inform what it was. But these ideals also came to be 'lived' by those carefully selected and *crafted* residents who called this place home. Here was the cultural logic of this community; one informed by the mutual creation of an image mediated from the fronts of signs and formulated in the *real* spaces and places of Greater Springfield's landscape.

What follows is an exploration of how ideals of community were packaged and presented via signage to the residents of this (sub)urban space, and more importantly, how these residents consumed, appropriated and resisted these.

The Fifteen-Foot-Tall Little Boy

Driving into Greater Springfield is an experience in itself. From the west (the direction from which I was always heading) the *Western Arterial Road* leads off from the *Centenary Highway*, cutting through remnant bushland to take the Springfield-bound traveller over a small rise and into Springfield Lakes. And there it is. From the elevated position of the road a glimpse of the lakes and the seemingly abundant watercourses (a rare commodity during the first decade of the development's history, in which below average rainfall and drought were a feature of life in south-east Queensland) lined by parklands and landscaped open space is offered; a clear visual cue as to the aesthetic arrangement of this manufactured place. By this stage of the journey, a dozen or more roadside signs offering visual and textual insights into Greater Springfield life have been passed—some of these not even located within the boundary of Greater Springfield itself. These ever-present physical manifestations of the underlying marketing campaigns attached to Greater Springfield's development signify such things as the *beauty, opportunity* and *lifestyle* available in this place, all the while branding the development in specific ways.

Even those neighbouring (and significantly less affluent, as it happens) suburbs that contained Greater Springfield's billboards and related signage stood as signifiers in and of themselves. These socio-economically depressed older suburbs stood in stark contrast to the glossy imagery of Greater Springfield. They offered a somewhat paradoxical experience in which the carefully composed and selected *everyday* moments of Greater Springfield life captured by the billboards contrasted against a backdrop that was significantly different. But Greater Springfield is after all an edge city, and this contrast of contexts is indeed a condition of the sort of development that is happening on the edges of south-east Queensland's urban sprawl.

Mention of Greater Springfield (particularly its two major sub-spaces, *Brookwater* and *Springfield Lakes*) is seemingly everywhere—or at least that's the impression the billboards provide. Perhaps it is due to the fanfare with which this new, technologically advanced development is met or the significant investment by its developers to make it a success that gives credence to the bombardment of the branding process. Or perhaps it is due to this location's edge city nature; a place built on the periphery of two other established cities that makes Greater Springfield an almost out-of-place place that exists largely because of the expansion of the urban fringe—a place thus requiring careful definition to demonstrate the uniqueness and identity it carries. In any case, the signs of Greater Springfield quickly emerged during my time there as being a prominent feature of the landscape; features that actively suggested much about what this place was intended to be.

Figure 9: A postmodern proverb urging me to reconsider my current life.
Photo; Andrew Hickey.

Figure 10: The sorts of discerning members intended for this community; a Brookwater resident clipping a lone, out-of-place blade of grass back into uniformity.
Photo: Andrew Hickey.

It was the frequency and the type of suggestions made by the signs that particularly caught my attention. The images they captured and the ideas they carried shot up out of the ground on the fronts of towering billboards that any visually aware person simply couldn't miss. The subjects caught casually posing within these portals into the cultural logic were particularly fascinating; a statement urging me to re-evaluate my current lot in life by considering the purchase of property in Greater Springfield (Figures 9 and 10); a 15-foot-tall little boy who beamed at me as he emerged from a swimming pool whilst advertising a 'cool change' at a revamped shopping centre (Figure 11); a 30-something couple relaxing in their studio apartment, whiling away a Sunday morning scene of comfortable relaxation (Figure 12).

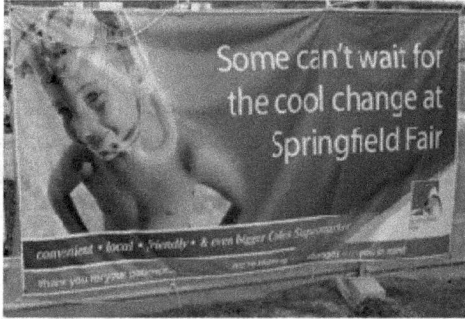

Figure 11: The fifteen-foot-tall little boy. Photo: Andrew Hickey.

Figure 12: A scene of domestic bliss and normality in Greater Springfield.
Photo: Andrew Hickey.

These signs carried an explicit purpose. They were telling me much about the place, but more importantly they also began telling me about who I could be if I moved into the area.

These images and their attached messages also appeared in other forms—'*Community Update*' newsletters, glossy corporate brochures and newspaper features—all distributed variously to residents, visitors and corporate partners of the development. These provided yet more suggestion of the type of lifestyle Greater Springfield yielded. Read alongside the billboards, these inter-supporting artifacts represented what it meant to be *in* Greater Springfield and provided textual affirmations of what the place was intended to be. Taken together, I realised that all of these artifacts of Greater Springfield provided a symbolic cultural road map for how to live there and behave appropriately as a resident.

Theming Greater Springfield

A range of ideals was attached to Greater Springfield and utilised in its marketing materials as branded attributes of the place. The overriding themes presented in the billboards derived broadly from the concept that Greater Springfield exists as a location in which residents can 'live-work-learn-play-shop' (Springfield Land Corporation 2005a). This often quoted[3] Greater Springfield catch phrase stands prominently as an articulation of the logic Greater Springfield's developers have given to the development's image.

Out of this concern for Greater Springfield to be a location that residents *don't ever need to leave*[4] are presented specific paleosymbolic ideals; including concerns for lifestyle, the availability of choice, the presence of community connectedness, a sense of belonging, opportunities for success and the convenience of local services. It is these underlying themes, expressed explicitly via authorising words or more subtly via the suggestions of imagery on billboards and other artifacts, that are important for understanding the cultural logic of Greater Springfield. These images and words actively framed what Greater Springfield was—what its 'logics' were. They shaped what the development became, and more significantly how people thought about it.

It was precisely the dissemination of these highly conceptualised and philosophical statements on living presented via things as mundane as roadside billboards that I found fascinating—a guidebook for living, read as you drove past. It was even more intriguing to note that for all the lofty idealism suggested by these themes, it was humble media that carried them— roadside signs. While this perhaps says more about contemporary methods of advertising than it does anything else, the sublimely visual nature of these massive roadside information disseminators and the supporting flyers, brochures and magazines that reinforced the message was hard to beat— particularly in terms of the romanticised images of suburban tranquillity and relaxed leisure these signs presented to anyone who happened to come into contact with them. All sorts of suggestions about identity, community and lifestyle were made within these static insights into Greater Springfield life.

Of course, the billboards that I was reading as a primary source of evidence in my ethnographic explorations formed an important element in

---

[3] This phrase has recurred frequently in speeches by representatives of the developers and numerous promotional documents from the Springfield Land Corporation.

[4] A theme several of my informants noted as being an attraction of life in Greater Springfield.

the marketing campaign deployed by the developers of Greater Springfield; namely the development giant *Delfin* and the *Springfield Land Corporation*. By their nature as objects of advertising, these signs were designed to present idealised views of what Greater Springfield *could* be; this I had to take account of. But the signs of Greater Springfield also did more than just display an idealised image of the place. They provided a basis upon which the cultural logic came to be set. Of course they were idealised, but they still *made sense*. They operated within the boundary of cultural sensibility, and for this reason stood as important manifestations of the cultural logic of the place. Here were public pedagogical artifacts that taken together suggested something not just about the way Greater Springfield had been conceptualised, but provided a set of identity characteristics for the people who lived there.

To explain this more fully, a survey of some of the more significant signs of Greater Springfield follows.

Springfield Lakes—What a Refreshing Change

The first, and most significant, set of signs displayed during my time in Greater Springfield was the Springfield Lakes specific *'What a Refreshing Change'*[5] series of lamp post banners. I first noticed these banners along *Springfield Lakes Boulevard* in the centre of the Springfield Lakes development (Figure 13). These banners presented a set of 'keywords'—authorising words that themed each banner's conceptual focus—with accompanying imagery and slogan containing a reference to the keyword and image and the generic *'what a refreshing change'* catch phrase.

This series included the following banners (in no particular order):

—*Community*
Keyword: Community.
Associated Slogan: Superb settings. What a refreshing change.
Imagery: Aerial view of a coffee shop gallery (Figure 14).

Using imagery depicting a moment captured on the deck of a prominent local Springfield Lakes coffee shop, this banner ties the idea of community with cosmopolitan consumerism and leisure; themes further conflated by the slogan 'superb settings'. The image on this banner shows a hint of the water of Springfield Lakes, as well as the leisurely but refined surroundings of the coffee shop deck. As a local landmark and popular location for socialising,

---

[5] As per the recurring slogan 'what a refreshing change' that appeared on all banners from this series.

the visual suggestion of the coffee shop set floating above the water of the lakes stands as a signifier of the social heart of Springfield Lakes—this suggestion is not only given credence by the geographic location of the coffee shop in central Springfield Lakes, but also via the symbolic, centralised meeting point this space functions as for locals.

Figure 13: The What a Refreshing Change banners in central Springfield Lakes. Photo: Andrew Hickey.

I take the banner keyword 'community' to here refer to a *sociable collectivity*. In this usage, community is about getting together with similar others (presumably other Springfield Lakes residents) to engage in relaxed conversation whilst admiring one of the 'superb settings' the place offers (*the lakes*, in this case). When I first looked at this banner in detail, I wondered what the subjects of this image were discussing; could they be engaged in Springfield-specific banter about shared points of interest of being *in* Springfield Lakes?[6] Were stories of life in Springfield Lakes shared, or details about the latest addition to the garden discussed or the success of a child at one of the local schools mentioned with quiet pride?

Regardless of what the subjects were indeed discussing, this was an image that seemingly captured an everyday moment (as all the banners in this series do) of what life in Greater Springfield *could be*. The point of course is that this everyday moment is in fact a bit spectacular; the fact that a seemingly everyday act as drinking coffee can occur in a 'superb setting' says something about this place and what it offers its residents. Here is a place where residents not only have time to sit leisurely sharing a sense of community with other like-minded folks but also do this amidst a backdrop

---

[6] As per Grange's (1999) suggestion that community is expressed as a shared response to the social world.

of stunning natural landscapes and an aesthetically pleasing built environment. The aerial perspective of the image is also interesting, and perhaps suggests something voyeuristic about the banner's viewer—here the viewer *looks in on* a seemingly typical moment of Springfield Lakes life. The viewer is presumably someone unfamiliar with the place (as the viewer needs to be told that this is in fact *community* in one of Springfield Lakes' *superb settings*), and is someone looking-in to understand its ways, perhaps with the intention of moving into the area (this is an advertisement designed to attract people to the development). It is from this perspective that a direct suggestion of desire permeates through the image—in this particular instance, a desire for relaxed sociability that residency in this 'superb setting' provides.

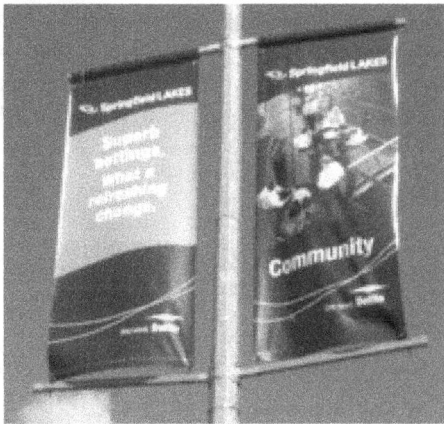

Figure 14: Community. Photo: Andrew Hickey.

—Conflating Themes of Community in Springfield Lakes

Community is a significant term in Greater Springfield. It refers not only to the way the area has been developed (that is, this location has been built as *the* community) but refers also to the type of interactions its residents have (that is, you become part of *a* community in which rich interpersonal relationships occur). A dual definition of community is expressed by this logic (particularly in Springfield Lakes and Brookwater), where community operates as an explicit keyword that signifies themes of interpersonal connectedness within the physical surroundings of the development.

Examples of this dual usage are expressed in the following:

1. *Community as location*:

> Springfield Lakes is a fully master planned community, designed with

> you in mind. Every detail has been thoroughly planned to help you enjoy every aspect of your life. (Delfin *Living Options* Magazine, Green Issue, n.d.)

> Springfield Lakes is a magnificent community that offers you every reason to enjoy your life the way you want to... how refreshing. (Delfin *Living Options Magazine*, Green Issue, n.d.)

2.   *Community as interpersonal relationships*:

> We will supply the vision and the design but it is the community that will make it a success. (Maha Sinnathamby, *The Big Picture, Health Special* November–December 2006)

> What makes Springfield Lakes truly unique is the strong community spirit. There are over 40 community groups operating within Springfield Lakes as well as the Spring Lake Community Centre that assists in fostering a sense of belonging within the vibrant Springfield Lakes Community. (Paul Cochrane, Springfield Lakes the Place to Be, *Urban Development Review*, April 2007)

> It is so wonderful that the community is getting behind our concert, it really is community helping the community. (Angela Burdett, *The Satellite*, October 10, 2007)

Whilst community defined as personal interaction is an important element in the conceptualisation of Springfield Lakes, the conflation of community as an aspect of the built environment is also significant. In many ways, community occurs *because of* the built environment in these examples— community is hinged to the coffee shop overlooking the lakes in the banner imagery; it is built by the developers but 'made a success' when people move into it; it is in the 'superb settings' of Springfield Lakes that community occurs. What these readings of the paleosymbolic application of community in Greater Springfield implicitly suggest is that community is only possible because of the design and construction of the built environment. The implication of this suggestion being that this place is special as *a* community because of the careful and considered planning that the developers have given to it. In this regard, community isn't an organically produced expression of human interaction alone, but is a direct result of the planning and design conventions utilised in Springfield Lakes by its creators.

This is in many ways a new definition of community—if the definitions discussed by Cohen (2004) and Bauman (2001) carry any weight. The built environment in this usage is conceptualised as a conduit or catalytic shell from which human interactions flow. It might even be assumed that without this specific built environment and the considered planning undertaken by the developers, that community would in fact be impossible in this place. This is a community *that is* because of the type of planning and design utilised in its physical environment. This is important, because here is the first conflation of both the physical and symbolic aspects of Greater Springfield community. What I see being suggested in this is that everything is taken care of—everything from the construction of the built environment right down to the way community interaction will be prescribed in the types of special places it avails.

—*Choice*
Keyword: Choice.
Associated Slogan: Great land deals. What a refreshing change.
Imagery: Middle-aged couple looking out over a balcony from a multi story residential dwelling (Figure 15).

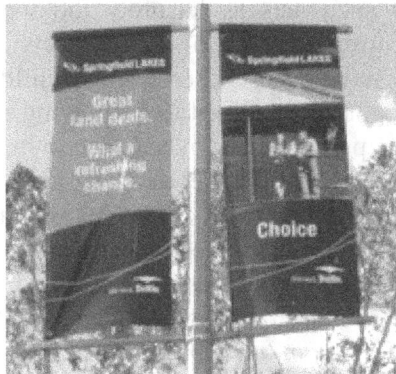

Figure 15: Choice. Photo: Andrew Hickey.

This banner utilised imagery of a couple looking out from a balcony of a multi story house, with accompanying slogan '*Great land deals. What a Refreshing Change*' ascribed on the side banner. Given that a representative of the marketing team of Springfield Land Corporation interviewed at the time mentioned that, where possible, subjects contained within publicity and marketing materials were Springfield residents, I have taken the assumption that the subjects contained in this image are residents and that the house is indeed located in Springfield:

They're actually Springfield Lakes residents that we use for all the

commercials, all the advertising is all Springfield Lakes residents.
(Nicole 28th March 2007)

I return to this later, as it is an important indicator of the ways that the development inculcated its own residents into the branding process. But for now, and apart from the bona fides of residency the subjects within the image may or may not claim, it is a theme of agency that carries through this banner. 'Choice', the underlying ideal of this sign, is further conflated with suggestions of *value* ('Great land deals') and *opportunity* (in terms of finding a suitable, well-priced home) in which happiness, leisure and relaxation are possible. This links closely to the 'refreshing change' motif that underlines the entire series of banners; here is a location that is refreshing not only because it is a place where community is present but where the opportunity to live comfortably is also made available.

What I find this banner suggesting is that, once you move to Springfield Lakes, you will have the choice of the home and lifestyle of your desire without spending every last dollar in the process, and will subsequently be able to enjoy life via such acts as leisurely looking out over your own balcony. Presumably, from the age of the subjects shown in the image, Springfield Lakes may have been chosen to raise children, who, outside the frame of the image, might be imagined to be playing across the road in one of the Springfield Lakes parks; a park over which mum and dad are 'keeping an eye'. With the themes 'Family', 'Belonging' and 'Learning' emerging from other banners in this series (as discussed below) an assumption that this is a place for families (perhaps even more specifically, young families) might be made.[7] This is certainly the suggestion presented in a Delfin-produced *Living Options* magazine distributed to residents of Springfield Lakes in 2005: *Imagine yourself living in a community focussed setting. Where people still smile at their neighbours and kids play safely in the park* (Delfin *Living Options*, Orange Issue, May 2005).

Apart from these suggestions of family, a restrained affluence is also presented as an expression of *Choice* in this banner. While great land deals will allow you to choose a large, comfortable and new house, there remains a corollary of modesty. Comfortable affluence, not opulence is the theme presented here, and by the brief snapshot of the house shown in the image, is signified by the type of house it is; by Greater Springfield standards this house very much represents an average Springfield Lakes residence. By extension to this reasoning, an economically derived class motif joins the

---

[7] From what I saw during my fieldwork and was told in interviews with residents of Springfield Lakes—discussed further in the next chapter—this is very much a major segment of the Springfield Lakes population.

signifier of age (*young* family) to present ideas of restrained affluence as a 'clever buy'. In this age of rising mortgages, the 'housing affordability crisis' (see Bartlett 2006; Silberberg 2007), expensive household commodities and transportation costs, the lifestyle that Springfield Lakes offers is one where working, living, playing and shopping become attractive to young families looking for affordable but comfortable environs to raise families. Here we have 'choice' coming to represent a thematic in which young families live an archetypal Australian lifestyle involving comfortable middle-class affluence, space to express a suburban identity and a place to play out the Australian dream.

—Conflating Themes of Choice in Springfield Lakes

The ideal of 'Choice', represented broadly as a type of agency where residents are provided options of housing and lifestyle, was subsequently also deployed in various other artifacts disseminated throughout Greater Springfield. Most prominent amongst these were the brochures and various Delfin-produced magazines that worked variously as carriers for lifestyle articles and property advertising. The articles in particular offered insights into the types of lifestyle one might lead in Springfield Lakes, as a suggestion in a *Living Options* magazine notes:

> Springfield Lakes is all about offering you options on how you want to live. From a huge range of housing choices through to choice of village addresses. Whatever your lifestyle, at Springfield Lakes you're sure to find the choice that's right for you. (Delfin *Living Options* Magazine, Orange Issue, n.d.)

This is furthered by the suggestion that in Springfield Lakes you can '*take a piece of land in a stunning location and build a home that suits your lifestyle*' (Delfin *Living Options* magazine, Orange Issue, n.d.).

The idea of choice also extends beyond housing options available to residents. It emerges in reference to such things as the availability of shopping centres and the provision of education. Here, choice equates as *variety* for consumers:

> Two shopping malls will be located in a beautifully landscaped setting, around a town square and a pedestrian-friendly main street. Offering many of the features of a traditional town centre, it will be a place to shop, eat out, meet friends, do business, and be entertained.... (*Education City News*, n.d.)

> Enabling students to enrol in Semester 2 [at the University of Southern Queensland] means that they do not have to wait...to begin their tertiary education.... For many programs we also offer three semesters, rather than

two, giving students the added flexibility of finishing their programs sooner, or spreading out their normal workloads to accommodate for work or family commitments. (Doug Fraser, interviewed in the Springfield Lakes *Catch Up* Magazine, Autumn 2007)

I found it interesting that Delfin's partners (including the University of Southern Queensland which developed a new campus in Education City) also drew on thematics such as choice to make their claims in the development. It is in this sense that these keywords extended beyond being simple marketing tools to represent a core attribute of the total development. These keywords represented the underlying philosophies—paleosymbolic ideals—for the development; philosophies that were similarly taken on by service providers (like the shopping centres and university) as much as they were by the developers themselves.

The ethic of choice presented in Springfield Lakes is perhaps summed up best by the following mission-statement-like suggestion, sourced from a Delfin-produced brochure:

> For Delfin, creating special places is not just a catchline—it's our lifeblood, our heritage and our vision. We're not in the business of building the ordinary. We change the face of the urban landscape, setting new standards in community development. **Creating special places where people can choose the way they live, the way they work, the way they learn and the way they play.** Springfield Lakes is a shining example. (Delfin *What a Refreshing Change* brochure, October 2006, *emphasis added*)

With this central concern for choice pronounced by the principal developer of the place, it is perhaps not surprising that *choice* features as an ideal in billboard representations of Springfield Lakes. This focus on choice might also be viewed against larger contextual features of the contemporary world; as a key component of market capitalism where consumer choice (espoused by processes of competition) stands as central to the logic of consumption, Springfield Lakes emerges (in these marketed images at least) as a place that is what you want it to be without costing you everything. Here you build your own place and engage in lifestyle choices catered to by the services available in Greater Springfield *at reasonable prices.*[8] As an ideal, choice operates as a point of distinction that defines Springfield Lakes according to what other urban developments don't (or can't) offer. Whether accurate or not, the suggestion is that Springfield Lakes provides choices for its residents to *live-work-learn-play-shop* as they see fit.

---

[8] This being of course another aspect of middle-class gentrification of the urban fringe.

—Belonging
Keyword: Belonging.
Associated Slogan: Heavenly homes. What a refreshing change.
Imagery: Mother, son and daughter laughing at a breakfast bar (Figures 16 and 17)

Connecting directly to the ideas presented in the 'Community' banner, but taking the idea of collectivity into personal space (that is, inside of the home environment), the 'Belonging' banner shows imagery of a family—or part thereof—sharing a seemingly happy moment of domestic everyday-ness. Clearly displayed are a young man (the son?), a middle-aged woman (the mother?) and less prominently, a young woman (the daughter?). Within this scene of indoor Springfield Lakes life, we see the older woman preparing food over a plate, whilst the younger people look on with smiling faces suggestive of family union and shared happiness. Here is imagery that suggests the sort of family structure Springfield Lakes residents might form.

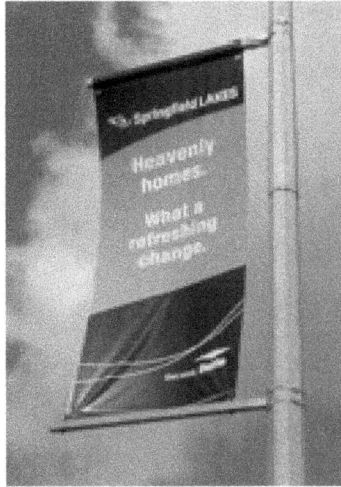

Figure 16: Belonging catch phrases. Photo: Andrew Hickey.

Missing in this image is an older male subject—we might have assumed a traditional nuclear family structure if one had been present—so we are left to speculate whether the 'dad' subject is at work (leaving mum to take care of the 'inside' domestic tasks) or that this is a single-parent family, with mum having maintained custody of the children (as is the case in the majority of single-parent families in Australia).

The supporting slogan '*Heavenly homes*' appears not to fit the image immediately, until consideration of the context in which this image of family happiness and belonging is set. The domestic satisfaction presented in the image is linked intrinsically to the home and more widely to the sense of satisfaction and belonging *heavenly* homes in Springfield Lakes bring. Just as with the 'Community' banner in which community is only possible in the master-planned environment of Springfield Lakes, it is implied that belonging is only possible due to the design and construction of Springfield Lakes houses. These are *houses that become homes* (to draw on the aphorism) because of the planning and type of construction used in Springfield Lakes.

This theme is further conflated with a second billboard (Figure 18) depicting 'Belonging' that was located on a major roadway on the western edge of Springfield Lakes from late 2006. In this, the idea of belonging is drawn from an image of children sharing an iconic childhood moment dipping toes into the lakes. This Tom Sawyer-like image, where childhood experience is symbolically expressed according to the water of the lakes (for Sawyer, this would be the Mississippi), connects the built environment of Springfield Lakes to iconic experiences of childhood, and more particularly for the banner themes above, the belonging that occurs due to the design and layout of Springfield Lakes' built environment.

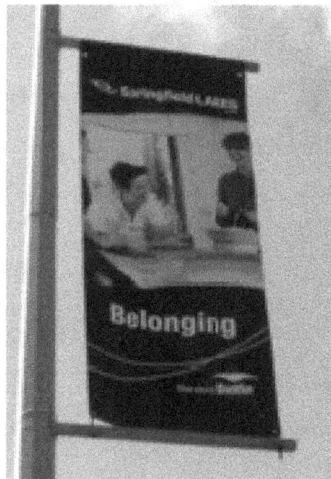

Figure 17: Belonging. Photo: Andrew Hickey.

The lakes, it needs to be remembered however, are artificial, with the rough hewn sandstone edges of the lake displayed in the image being just as manufactured as the houses that fill the development; each of these 'special places' is just as manufactured as the other, with any nostalgia or feigned history of these structures suggesting a pastiche (Jameson 1991). Similar imagery is deployed on the cover of a *Good Life* magazine (Figure 19), where the connection of the childhood experience is made according to the water of the lakes. Just as belonging is integrally connected to the *inside* built environment, it is also connected to the design and construction of the larger *outside* space of the development. Springfield Lakes is, just like your own private home, a place in which you *belong*.

—Conflating Themes of Belonging in Springfield Lakes

The most striking conflation of ideals that emerged from the various brochures and newsletters that were distributed during my time in Greater Springfield was the connection of the themes Belonging and Community. In many ways this makes sense—being in a community means feeling connected and belonging to it. But what is significant here is the continuation of the connection between the way Greater Springfield has been designed and the possibility for belonging this prescribes:

> Belonging. Have you ever been welcomed to a new community where you're invited to join in and get to know the people and the places a little better? At Springfield Lakes, regular community events enable you to do just that. (Delfin *What a Refreshing Change* brochure, n.d.)

> It's easy to belong at Springfield Lakes. The best part is, there are so many other groups and clubs you can belong to at Springfield Lakes. (Delfin *What a Refreshing Change* brochure, n.d.)

Figure 18: Belonging conflated. Photo: Andrew Hickey.

It is again the underlying suggestion regarding the way that Springfield Lakes has been constructed that is significant. As with the themes emerging from the 'Community' banner, where the built environment and the nature of its construction stand as catalytic elements underpinning the function of community, belonging too seems to be hinged on the way the development has been crafted. In Springfield Lakes, all residents need do is come and be *belonged*. The physical environment upon which interpersonal human connections are placed is all set up waiting for residents to feel part of it all.

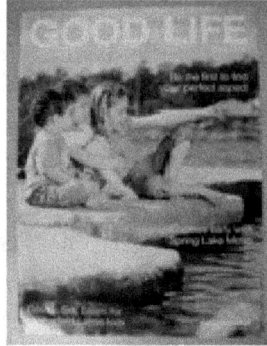

Figure 19: Belonging deployed. Photo: Andrew Hickey.

A prime example of this pre-formed expression of belonging is further suggested by an advertisement for the Orion Shopping and Entertainment Precinct. In a small cardboard brochure containing a magnetic strip on the back designed to be placed on a refrigerator in the home, the cover headline ran "Merry Christmas from Your Newest Neighbour" followed by the line: "Orion Springfield…we look forward to seeing you at our place in the new year" (Orion Springfield Opening brochure, June 2007). Apart from the concerns one might have with the gesture of a shopping centre welcoming residents of Greater Springfield to its 'place' (in some attempt to make blatant consumerism homely), a key expression of how belonging is worked into (and in this case dependent upon) the built environment and its design is expressed here. Via this welcoming gesture by a shopping centre an authorisation of belonging is made to residents. Rather than being the proverbial home made cake brought over by the neighbours as the move into the new Springfield Lakes home occurs, belonging in this example is mediated by a consumerist logic, where corporations function just like individuals in this master-planned context (Harvey 2005:77). Under this logic, to belong to the community of Greater Springfield means having a connection to its institutions (such as its shopping centres); the extension of this being that belonging means being welcomed into a consumerist logic, which suggests much about the type of living Springfield Lakes residents are required to lead.

—*Home*
Keyword: Home.
Associated Slogan: Easy living. What a refreshing change.
Imagery: Sunset view over Springfield Lakes foregrounded with a runner and cyclist (Figure 20).

Just as with the 'Belonging' banner, the imagery and keyword presented on this banner don't quite seem to correlate at first glance. However it is the juxtapositioning of the keyword 'Home' against an image depicting a sunrise on the lakes that connects ideas of home to the larger community context of Springfield Lakes. Just as with the imagery contained in the 'Belonging' banner where ideas of belonging were located in a specific context of the social milieu (inside the family home), this banner identifies ideas of home as they pertain to the larger 'outside' space of Springfield Lakes.

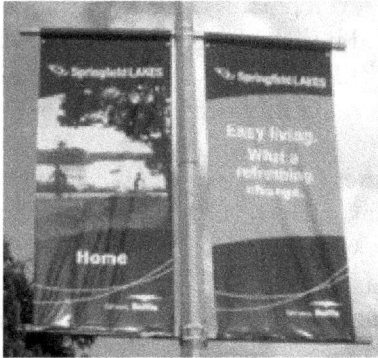

Figure 20: Home. Photo: Andrew Hickey.

That is to say, that while you may indeed own a house in Greater Springfield, it is in fact the whole place that is actually *home*. From this, a thematic correlation to the ideas presented in other banners emerges, in which ideas of personal safety, belonging, leisure and a general sense of lifestyle are linked directly to the entire Springfield Lakes space. It is not just your own privately owned house and block that matter, but the suburb *en masse*.

Again, the landmark lakes and surrounding parkland function as a signifier of where home is in the image. As the spiritual and geographic centre of Springfield Lakes, the lakes present a space where 'easy living' might occur, as the slogan suggests. Here again, it is suggestions of leisure, relaxation and comfort that are presented—particularly in the form of the active and vibrant-looking residents exercising in the foreground of the imagery.

—Conflating Themes of Home in Springfield Lakes

Suggestions of home, when applied in the brochures and other artifacts, generally didn't apply this suburb-wide usage of the term. Invariably, home referred to privately owned residences:

> Introducing the new Springfield Lakes Gallery Collection, architectural
> splendour providing huge street appeal. These chic new homes offer the
> ultimate in low maintenance lifestyle not to mention individuality. These
> freehold homes are located in prime positions to ensure you get the best
> proximity to everything at Springfield Lakes. Parks, ovals, lakes, hike and
> bike trails and facilities are at your doorstep making for a relaxed and easy
> lifestyle. (Delfin 'Gallery Collection' Sales brochure, n.d.)

With the exception of a 'postcard' style advertising flyer that suggested that
the 'Lakes Entrance' development 'is truly a place you can call home',
mention of home referred invariably to private residences solely.

In some ways this still fits the definition of home laid out in the street
banner. While we see a reference to home as the entire space of Springfield
Lakes in the banner (a collective home), it is the way that the space
accommodates the privately owned *house-as-home* that is significant in other
artifacts. While you may own a house in Springfield Lakes, it becomes a
home due to its location within the wider Springfield Lakes community. Here
home is a concept that connects directly with ideas of Community and
Belonging, and carries underlying themes of lifestyle, choice and style.

The beauty of Springfield Lakes, as the advertising suggests, is that it
allows you to live your life according to your style:

> Aspect—Springfield Lakes Latest Address—Your Life, Your Home, Your
> Style. Aspect at Springfield Lakes delivers a lifestyle offering to the
> discerning homebuyer, with a combination of natural surrounds in a
> convenient location. (Delfin *Living Options* Magazine, Green Issue, n.d.)

Ideas of the home directly correlate with the lifestyle you are able to lead. By
this logic the house is an 'address' that is made a home according to the
lifestyle you are provided with. It is within this suburb-wide home that a
lifestyle is lived, with leisure, activity, style and a 'good life' available to all
who choose one of the addresses within it:

> Lakeside—live the good life by the water. The Lakeside experience begins
> the moment you are greeted by the breathtaking sight of Spring Lake. It
> continues down leafy Springfield Lakes Boulevard, over the bridge and
> through the grand entrance that marks your arrival. **It's a magical welcome
> home that you *could* be experiencing everyday.** (Delfin *Living Options*
> Magazine, Green Issue, n.d., *emphasis added*)

Choice features as an important sub-theme within these suggestions. In the
pre-formed space of Springfield Lakes, where specific types of home are

accorded specific sections of the development, choice is ultimately limited, yet the idea of choosing a home that fits your lifestyle presents as a prominent ideal in the imagery. You may well have a choice between the 'Gallery Homes' of the 'Parkside' development or the 'high quality addresses at realistic prices' of Lakes Entrance, but ultimately choice is limited to a specific aesthetic and stylistic form of housing; the brick and tile/steel-roofed self-contained house. I can't help but wonder what would happen in Springfield Lakes if your *choice* happened to preference life in a communal long-house, or an open-plan warehouse. It is unlikely that Springfield Lakes could accommodate these choices. It is perhaps even more unlikely that prospective residents would even consider such choices when confronted with the brochures detailing what sorts of houses are available.

This usage of choice makes the suggestion about the 'Aspect' development all that more intriguing (Figure 21):

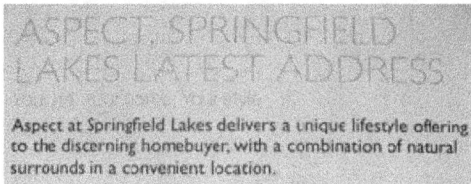

ASPECT, SPRINGFIELD
LAKES LATEST ADDRESS

Aspect at Springfield Lakes delivers a unique lifestyle offering to the discerning homebuyer, with a combination of natural surrounds in a convenient location.

Figure 21: 'Aspect' and its brand of living. Photo: Andrew Hickey.

Rather than reading 'your life, your home, your style', perhaps the slogan might more correctly read as 'your life, your home, your style, *as long as your ideas of housing happen to fit with what we've built*'. I argue that this example is a key expression of not only what types of home are considered appropriate in Springfield Lakes, but by extension, what type of people are expected to live here according to the options of style that are made available. It is indeed the built environment that influences the sorts of lifestyles that can be led against the versions of the suburban home that are provided. As a point at which choice manifests in a physical form, the homes of Springfield Lakes function in this regard as informal stylistic sorting devices for prospective residents. If your idea of suburban living is captured by the choice of houses made available, then Springfield Lakes is for you. If the 'choices' don't align with your ideas, move along.

—*Family*
Keyword: Family.
Associated Slogan: Your choices. What a refreshing change.
Imagery: Man and girl sitting in a park (Figure 22).

The second banner to contain imagery of domestic connectivity, 'Family' utilises imagery of a man (a father?) and a young girl (a daughter?). But unlike the suggestions of the family unit deployed in the 'Belonging' banner, this version of family occurs outside. The suggestion here seems to be that the outside constitutes a male space—a theme that complements the female *inside* space of the 'Belonging' banner.

The application of an outdoor setting in this banner also carries themes of safety (the open parks are safe for a young family to casually play and bond), leisure (again, Springfield Lakes provides the right sort of spaces for relaxation and family connection) and special places (this is a scene depicting one of Springfield Lakes' idyllic parklands—landmark features of the area).

Figure 22: Family. Photo: Andrew Hickey.

What Springfield Lakes provides, as suggested by this banner, is a location where 'choices' are available—choices of how to live, how to spend leisure time and how to bond with family and community. Add to this the determinant 'your' in the 'your choices' slogan, and a clear indication of personal agency is added to the mix. Springfield Lakes, as this banner suggests, is a place in which *you* can choose to do what *you* wish, and more importantly, has the resources and 'special places' to allow *you* to fulfil these activities (including such places as convenient shopping centres, family-oriented parklands and community-minded coffee shops).

—Conflating Themes of Family in Springfield Lakes

Family constitutes a core component of the conceptualisation of Greater Springfield, and in Springfield Lakes specifically, signifies the basic unit of social organisation; it is *the* Family that re-occurs as a theme in Greater Springfield when collective union is noted in the various artifacts. Whilst mention of the individual is also frequent, the implicit suggestion is that these people reside with their families and live in Greater Springfield's homes in this type of social grouping. This is a specific application of the term, as it isn't used to describe larger networks (as in a *Springfield Lakes family* for instance; these sorts of collectives are signified by words like *community*, or more vaguely via the themes suggested by the 'Belonging' keyword). Family in the applications taken from the artifacts refers directly to a nuclear family of genealogically connected individuals; typically a very traditional Australian family network of 'mum, dad and the kids'.

An example of this is seen in the way that Orion Shopping Centre identifies the family as one of its core demographics:

> Your Town Centre has the family covered. At Orion Springfield we have a range of services to suit your family's needs. (*Springfield News*, April 18, 2007)

This example also provides an expression of how community relates back to and is engaged by the family. We see services within the development mobilized in terms of family life, which subsequently positions the family centrally as the basic unit of social organisation:

> Family ties are close to home. Three brothers and a sister are living the vision of Greater Springfield's founder Maha Sinnathamby—to work, live and play in the area. Jo Ribes and her brothers Paul, Mark and Steve Hodgson love the convenience of working close to home. 'I could have moved close to the city or set up a business here and this is such a nice place to live that it makes more sense working close to home'. While family ties play a role, the four also say living and working locally makes good business sense. (*Springfield News*, April 18, 2007)

Apart from the underlying economic themes that ideals of family are infused with in this example (*'working locally also makes good business sense for this family'*), this application of Family and the Springfield Lakes experience draws on several underlying themes to make its case. Firstly, the 'your choices' slogan noted on the banner suggests that ways of living, prosperity, convenience and belonging don't require distance from those closest to you; in Springfield Lakes, *Family* is in fact a core component of the entire logic of the place upon which leisure, special places, belonging and other keywords and slogans are premised. With the family operating as the conceptualisation of how people and the social landscape are structured, we see the mediation of the built environment, types of housing, range of services and amenities such as schools and parkland offered in Greater Springfield reflecting this type of social group. These themes certainly pervade the following section of a brochure advertising the entire Greater Springfield development:

> Greater Springfield is a self-contained community unlike any other in south-east Queensland. The focus on maintaining a healthy lifestyle—which includes a careful balance between work and family—underlies the growing community. And it is this focus that has attracted families who place a strong emphasis on quality of life from school age to retirement. (Delfin *Greater Springfield from Vision to Reality* brochure, n.d.)

Just as with the 'Choice' banner, where choices of homes were shown as a hallmark feature of the development, but from which a very particular aesthetic and style of housing is actually offered, I can't help but wonder how the banner imagery and notions of Family suggested by it would cope with a non-traditional, or non-Western family structure. In any event, we simply don't see *those* sorts of families presented by the artifacts.

From the organisation of suburban developments in the physical landscape to the focus the shopping centres give in their marketing materials, family represents a conceptualisation of how social structures are organised at their core; it is a nuclear family that represents how people arrange themselves in Greater Springfield. It is then no surprise to see the types of houses that are built, the way that public space is configured and the nature of the pastimes and leisure pursuits provided in Greater Springfield; with the representation of the *standard* family unit being that of the nuclear family representations that support this follow, including imagery of contemporary versions of the archetypal Australian brick veneer family home, parklands in which family picnic lunches and childhood experiences of the lakes might occur and shopping centres that provide for the procurement of family needs in our consumerist world.

—*Learning*
Keyword: Learning.
Associated Slogan: A bright outlook. What a refreshing change.
Imagery: Primary-aged students walking to school (Figure 23).

With the Education City development and local schools and learning centres situated as a major feature of the Greater Springfield master plan, learning and education are presented as integral themes in the development. This particular banner captures this concern, but also suggests much about what 'type' of education is considered important in Springfield Lakes. The type of education represented is very much 'formal' and school oriented—in this specific instance, a depiction of students from a local private school in which learning relates to processes of schooling represented in a *traditional* way via the signifiers of school uniforms and bags attached to young people.

Figure 23: Learning. Photo: Andrew Hickey.

Beyond this identification of the type of learning that occurs in Springfield Lakes is the aspirational nature of the accompanying slogan; 'A bright outlook'. Learning isn't deployed solely for the 'furnishing of the mind', but offers opportunity for success. Here opportunity as a 'bright outlook' presumably refers to a successful education that translates into a good job, money and the ability to compete in a highly competitive capitalist world. The remarkable feature of this banner is the juxtapositioning of the young girls in the image and the extent to which their futures are mapped by the suggestions of the slogan. Learning and the girls' futures go hand in hand as concurrent concerns.

—Conflating Themes of Learning in Greater Springfield

The investment and allocation of space to learning is a fundamentally important aspect of Greater Springfield's development. Maha Sinnathamby regularly identifies his philosophy for education via columns in the *Springfield Times*[9], various Delfin and Springfield Land Corporation newsletters and during a meeting with the then prime minister of Australia, John Howard, that I was fortunate enough to be part of:

---

[9] Through 2005 and into early 2006 as the development in Springfield Lakes was taking shape, Maha Sinnathamby had a regular column in this newspaper discussing a variety of topics including the significance of family connectedness, sustainable urban planning and progress in the Greater Springfield developments, amongst other topics.

> Mr Prime Minister, we are heavily committed to this project…and what this
> project is doing is uplifting the society very rapidly… One of the unique
> features of this development is that you have all forms of education, from
> early childhood to tertiary. (Education City Opening, Meeting with Prime
> Minister John Howard, 19th April, 2006)

Sinnathamby repeated similar themes in a speech delivered to invited guests
at the official opening of the Education City development:

> It is through education alone that we can uplift our society and challenge the
> fast growing world we are in. To educate everyone from infant to adulthood
> is the best gift one can give to an individual. From a commercial point it is
> the best investment a nation can make. (Education City Opening Speech, 19th
> April, 2006)

The importance of education is also acknowledged by other significant
people in the region, with the mayor of Ipswich also commenting on the
value of education to Greater Springfield as integral to the future prosperity
of the region and its people:

> When you look around and see the important role that knowledge and the
> knowledge industry play in our community it makes you feel very proud
> because it means that our children and their children, and the residents of
> today are going to have a future here through education…we've embraced
> education as a vital component of everything we're trying to achieve. (Paul
> Pisassale, Education City Opening, 19th April, 2006)

The logic underpinning each of these comments positions education as a tool
to equip residents for the future. Implicated within this are notions of social
capital that see prosperity and socio-economic development hinged on the
knowledge generation that education provides. In these quotes, the socially
transformative potential of education carries a larger imperative; education is
exalted as something that dictates the future success of the entire region and
not just those individuals who seek to be educated.

While I agree with the social justice implications the suggestions by
Maha Sinnathamby and Paul Pisassale carry, the perceived outcomes of this
education system are interesting. Particularly with Sinnathamby's
suggestions, education functions as a *good investment*; one that ensures
prosperity via the competitive edge educational opportunity in Greater
Springfield seemingly provides. Education is far more than just the
furnishing of the mind; a prestigious pasttime for those with time and money
to spend picking up *tid-bits* of interesting knowledge. Education is a

necessity in a competitive, market-driven knowledge society.

It is via this logic of education as a component of a market-driven social context that an indication of how education is conceived emerges. As conveyed above, education is viewed primarily according to the type of learning (lifelong learning from 'early childhood to tertiary' as Sinnathamby noted) that occurs in early learning centres, schools and universities specifically. As such, I suggest that the *brand* of education presented in Greater Springfield should more correctly be labelled 'schooling'; it is that form of education and learning that occurs within prescribed institutional locations:

> Educational facilities are state of the art. From childcare, private and public schools, through to the University of Southern Queensland's Springfield Campus, every stage of learning is catered for at Springfield Lakes. What's more, construction has also commenced on the new Springfield Lakes State School, due to open in 2007. (Delfin *Living Options* Magazine, Orange Issue, n.d.)

What this vision of education doesn't include are those informal processes of learning that occur organically in Greater Springfield—processes which are indeed the subject of this book. It might be assumed that education (as the representations presented by the artifacts suggest) is about building social order via very formalised and prescribed mechanisms; little indication of education and learning pertaining to informal processes of peer mentoring, community networking or the influence of signage, for instance, are present. According to the imagery, education is synonymous with schooling and it is only within these formal locations of education that learning in Greater Springfield is understood to occur.

—Perfect Packages
Keyword: No keyword.
Associated Slogan: Perfect packages. What a refreshing change.
Imagery: No imagery (Figure 24).

A single-sided banner without imagery was used to advertise house and land packages for sale in Springfield Lakes. This banner bookended the others within the series and was located at the end of the row of banners on Springfield Lakes Boulevard. The concept of perfection is notable here—it's as if all of these banners, coming together as a conceptual amalgam of Springfield Lakes' ideals, culminate in this one suggestion. It might also be that these packages also contain the private-public dynamics of having 'packaged' shopping experiences on your doorstep, of having leisure activities as a central part of the Springfield Lakes experience and the ability to connect leisure, life, work and play in the one space. It remained that what Springfield Lakes *was*, as presented by its developers, was *perfection* divided up neatly into 600m2 blocks.

Figure 24: Perfect packages. Photo: Andrew Hickey.

The ideal suggested by this banner is a somewhat pretentious statement to make—that social and architectural residential perfection is achieved in Springfield Lakes is a bold point to claim. But I argue that this claim also says something about the residents of the place. In many ways, if you aren't happy here, *there must be something wrong with you*, as the packages that you move into are indeed themselves *perfect*. Here is a suggestion about the nature of this place and the formative influence it exerts figuratively over its residents who are expected to fit into its neatly subdivided blocks.

—Conflating Themes of Perfection in Greater Springfield

In the artifacts gathered during my time in Greater Springfield, the idea of perfection was largely conflated with themes of lifestyle. An inset quote in a full-page image of a young woman arranging flowers taken from a Delfin sales brochure (Figure 25) captures this intent:

> We found our perfect lifestyle at Springfield Lakes. (Delfin *What a Refreshing Change* brochure, October 2006)

Drawing on similar ideals, an advertisement for 'Aspect' development suggested:

> Aspect at Springfield Lakes is the perfect address to enjoy your life, your home, your style, your way. (Delfin *Good Life* Magazine, Spring 2006)

Figure 25: The 'perfect' lifestyle. Photo: Andrew Hickey.

A suggestion of agency is raised in this example. Springfield Lakes works as a complementary location that supports 'your' way of living and provides a foundation upon which lifestyles can be led. But given the pre-formed nature of the Greater Springfield development it could be assumed that the lifestyles that are indeed led are similarly pre-formed and set within certain constraints. As such, the implicit suggestion of choice that underpins this thematic of perfection really only applies to those who are happy to live a suburban, brick-veneered residential lifestyle set on a 600m2 block. An informal selection process of sorts is in operation here, with the suggestion of perfection applying equally to the sorts of people who will move here and fit in with the sorts of lifestyle and housing choices available. In these otherwise perfect places it becomes the responsibility of the resident to live up to these ideals of perfection and lead lifestyles that fit the logic of the surroundings. I can't help but read these suggestions of perfection on a couple of levels; firstly, in terms of the implied suggestions they make of the quality of the built environment and general aesthetic of Greater Springfield, and secondly, according to the demands it places on those people who move into this *perfect* place.

The Series

I took this series to be largely representative of the underlying logic of Springfield Lakes as seen by its developers. These were after all marketing tools that encapsulated a particular, but authorised, view of the place. Within the suggestions of each banner sat a symbolic blueprint for what life *could* be like in Greater Springfield. But it was the way specific ideals were included as expressive of life in Springfield Lakes that was of particular interest. The way that family units were visualised, the way that leisure activities were performed, the way that ideas of happiness and philosophies of living were presented suggested something more than just the dynamics of living in Greater Springfield. These blueprints for living in Greater Springfield tapped into a far deeper logic—one I suggest carries the concerns of many late-capitalist urban developments (as expressed throughout the entire series whereby contemporary lifestyles like the ones to be lived in Greater Springfield unquestioningly require mortgages, certain styles of housing, an education for that 'competitive edge' and shopping). I found it particularly interesting that far from identifying anything alternative, these banners wholeheartedly maintained, and presented as desirable, lifestyles that fitted the logic of Western capitalism. Very 'standard' ways of living were depicted within these visions of Greater Springfield life. But again, I had to remind myself that these artifacts were advertisements; advertisements that were generated by the system they supported.

It was the integrated nature of this series of banners that was particularly significant. Not just in terms of the integration of ideas and themes between each of the banners in this series, but the connection they yielded to other artifacts presented in Greater Springfield. Here was a manufacturing of the logic of Greater Springfield; an attempted construction of what the epistemology of this place was to be. So it went that the themes presented in the banners were redeployed in accompanying marketing materials, with the effect being a multimedia presentation of ideals that were hard to avoid— part of the 'marketing mix' that contemporary advertisers understand too well. From the visually dominant roadside reminders of what Springfield Lakes *is* grew further reinforcement of the same ideas in magazines, newspaper articles, flyers and other artifacts.

This series gave prominence to the 'refreshing-ness' of Greater Springfield by drawing close attention to its vitality as a new urban space. In the *What a Refreshing Change* series of banners and the associated artifacts, a symbolic suggestion of how the community *works* was presented. This is a place in which front doors of houses supposedly didn't form a border to collective life, where shopping malls were as important as a local coffee shop or parkland for spending time with family and friends and a pretence of choice featured as a marker of distinction and an expression of one's lifestyle.

When I looked at the banners and the associated artifacts, I noticed important paleosymbolic themes emerge. Firstly, there was a type of agency manifesting as 'choice' that permeated the entire logic of Springfield Lakes. This presented as the ability residents had to live as they wished. Next, leisure emerged as an opportunity to spend quality time with family and friends in the 'special places' of Springfield Lakes. Happiness and fulfillment connected to this, but these ideals were distinguishable according to the belonging that community gave and the opportunity to learn, shop and enjoy the services that were locally available. Finally, it emerged that the basic unit of social organisation in Springfield Lakes was the family, and it was from this that the design of its houses, parklands, shopping centres and education providers was derived. Under the logic presented by these paleosymbols emerged the entire vision of Springfield Lakes.

Find Your Uplifting Place

This series of billboards was first displayed along *Springfield Parkway*, a major roadway leading up a small rise to the *Escarpment* development on the northern edge of Springfield Lakes. Apart from signifying the elevated position of the Escarpment and surrounding villages the signs led to, the idea of being 'uplifted' featured heavily in Greater Springfield during my time there. Apart from being deployed on a set of billboards located on a busy thoroughfare, the theme also featured explicitly in a range of other marketing artifacts (most prominently in the form of marketing flyers presented as community newsletters) and more implicitly in speeches and public announcements delivered by the development's creator; Maha Sinnathamby. While I'm not suggesting that Sinnathamby wasn't simply supporting his own marketing machine by using the catch phrases and slogans from the campaign in his own rhetoric, the smoothly embedded mention of Springfield Lakes as an 'uplifted' place cross-marketed this series of banners very effectively. One key example of this was witnessed in a speech delivered during the opening of the Education City development:

> ...when this land was first offered to the marketplace, nobody wanted to buy it because it was in an area that was socially and economically very depressed, and what this project is doing is **uplifting** the society very rapidly... One of the unique features of this development is that you have all forms of education, from early childhood to tertiary. (Maha Sinnathamby, Speech delivered at the Education City Official Opening, 19th April, 2006, *emphasis added*)

Sinnathamby continued by connecting his personal philosophy of education to the ideals of uplifted-ness, suggesting that it was via the services provided in Greater Springfield (its education facilities in this instance) that residents could achieve success. To be uplifted in Sinnathamby's ideal meant having a comfortable home, convenient places to shop, a choice of places to study and the opportunity to live a lifestyle in the carefully manufactured space of

Greater Springfield. To come to Greater Springfield meant leaving behind something lesser to embrace a renewed, *higher* level of lifestyle.

An indication as to what living in Greater Springfield meant was also delivered by this series of billboards. This new series added a further definition to the lifestyles available; it wasn't enough to be simply offered *choices* or *opportunities*. These attributes were now also shown as being *uplifting* for residents. Something greater than that presumably available in other suburban developments was presented in Springfield Lakes. What the marketers were trying to say of course is that Springfield Lakes was that little bit better than anything else around.

The Billboards

The billboards themselves were simple enough. As with the street banners in the '*What a refreshing change*' series, a combination of imagery and authorising words were deployed to present the meaning of the billboard. But unlike the former series, the authorising words weren't as prescriptive, with the imagery assuming a greater role in making the billboards' suggestions. A different level of interpretation to that applied with the street banners of the previous series was required by the viewer given the primarily visual nature of these billboards. Far more reading of the image was required—a more *emotional* connection was perhaps warranted than that required by the authorising words of the '*What a refreshing change*' series of banners.

The series opened with a generically sloganed '*Find Your Uplifting Place*' billboard (Figure 26) with accompanying imagery of a young girl playing with bubbles set against a backdrop of towering native eucalypt trees (the same trees that were largely cleared to make way for the development, only to be regrown in the faux-natural watercourses and parklands).

I read the key suggestion in this billboard to be one of a *choice* (presented as personal agency); to identify and interact with places that are significant to the individual. The underlying suggestion here is that residents can find, and make meaningful, the special places of Springfield Lakes.

Figure 26: Find your uplifting place. Photo: Andrew Hickey.

Drawn into this thematic is a recognition that places are *spaces that are invested with meaning*; locations that are transformed into something meaningful via phenomenological investment of personal ideals. As with the *'What a Refreshing Change'* series of banners, the implication of this meaning-making process is the suggestion that the space of Springfield Lakes has been constructed as something significant by the developers. A suggestion of gentrification is presented here, where the land 'that nobody wanted to buy', as noted by Sinnathamby in his speech to the prime minister and guests, had been transformed into something that people might now find uplifting. As part of the marketing 'spin' that represents the transformative developmental work of the developers as something to be celebrated, the reconfiguration of this previously economically depressed region according to a middle-class aesthetic is seen as something natural and positive. Even the local newspaper—an entity not connected to the developers—celebrated this process of urban renewal:

> Growth Corridor... **The turning of empty land into the buildings blocks of Springfield** under the visionary leadership of Maha Sinnathamby has been a singular success, with tens of thousands of people expected to move in over the next 20 years. (*Springfield News*, 24th October 2007, *emphasis added*)

The cynic in me reads this praise as being reminiscent of Maoist Chinese propaganda—*the 'visionary leadership' of Chairman Maha* (he is indeed the *Chairman* of the Springfield Land Corporation) is too easy a comparison to make!

But for whom this transformation was uplifting becomes an immediate question; particularly in terms of how it has taken place. According to whose image and interests has this previously 'economically very depressed' place been transformed? I suspect that it isn't those former residents whose socio-economic circumstance has meant that they are now locked out of this market (this is an expensive place to live after all).

I similarly imagine that it wasn't in the interests of the traditional custodians of the land, the *Jaggera* people, who in a somewhat strange irony were present at the various openings of buildings and sections of the development and provided a 'welcome to country'—their country, upon which was built a middle-class dream, that, due to the legacy of colonial oppression, means that they will be unlikely to be residents. In this instance at least, I suggest that the marketing campaign moved beyond being simple advertising to become suggestive of something bigger. Here was the construction of a logic from within which people identified themselves and from which their relative economic status provided a selection criterion from which the 'choice' to live in Springfield Lakes was made. As such, this series of billboards said so much more than *how nice* Springfield Lakes was. Tied up within it was an entire logic of who could live here and how they would do it. This was identity politics displayed 10 metres in the air from the fronts of billboards.

But How to Become Uplifted?

The remaining billboards in this series each suggested a specific attribute. Suggested primarily by the imagery of each billboard, but contextualized by the accompanying text, suggestions of health and wellness, active lifestyle, choice, leisure, learning, comfort and convenience were presented. As I noted above, many of these themes connected with the earlier '*What a Refreshing Change*' series; but here was something more specific.

To 'power up' (Figure 27) means to achieve physically within the beautiful natural surrounds of Greater Springfield where walking and bicycle tracks are available to stay fit and well. The celebratory pose of the subjects caught posing in this seemingly normal Greater Springfield scene suggests something about a feat of accomplishment being achieved. It may even be that these subjects are competitive, over-achievers arrogantly thrusting their bicycles skyward as they 'power up' to celebrate this latest victory. These are presumably people who would also achieve in other aspects of life (the ideal Springfield Lakes resident, perhaps).

To 'grow up' (Figure 28) refers to learning and *uplifting* oneself through educational success. Here, a sense of maturity is suggested via the furnishing of the mind that Greater Springfield's education facilities and *Education City* precinct provides.

To 'catch up' (Figure 29) refers to spending leisure time doing things one enjoys (as signified by the family dog catching a *Frisbee* in its mouth—I can imagine that 'the kids' and possibly even the neighbours are just out of frame in this image, perhaps enjoying a barbeque in one of Greater Springfield's parks on an archetypal 'Sunday afternoon').

Figure27: Power up. Photo: Andrew Hickey.

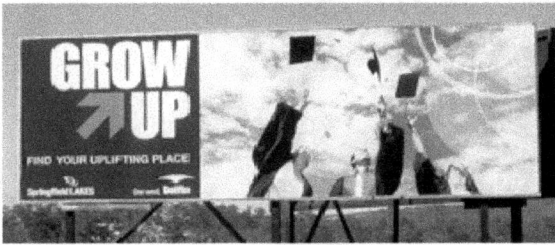

Figure 28: Grow up. Photo: Andrew Hickey.

'Eat Up' (Figure 30) carries connection to Greater Springfield's shopping centres and the availability of choice in selecting and purchasing produce to match one's gastronomic needs. In this billboard, shopping is connected directly to the Springfield Lakes experience—this time referring to the gastronomic aspects of lifestyle.

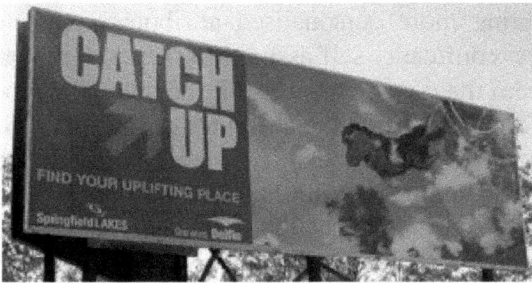

Figure 29: Catch up. Photo: Andrew Hickey.

Finally, 'move up' (Figure 31) carries themes of lifestyle, implicated by a suggestion of *class-as-distinction*. To move up in Springfield Lakes means having something a little more exclusive than the rest of the world—in this instance, time for relaxed leisure spent within a modern and expansive home set amongst a leafy backdrop.

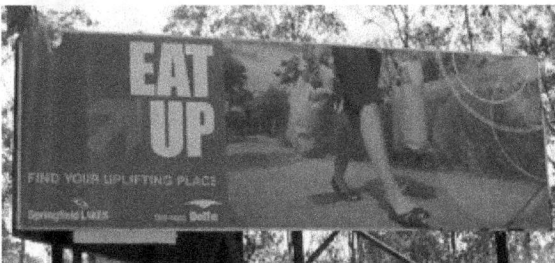

Figure 30: Eat up. Photo: Andrew Hickey.

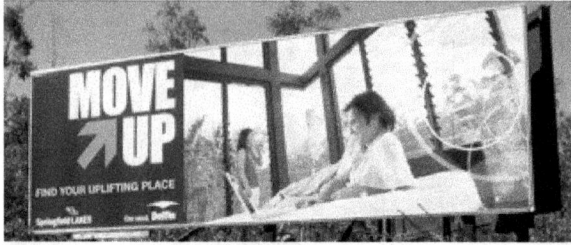

Figure 31: Move up. Photo: Andrew Hickey.

Conflating the Billboards of the 'Find Your Uplifting Place' Series

Given that this series of billboards appeared after the *'What a Refreshing Change'* series of banners, I have read it to respond to and fill in the gaps presented in the ideals the banners portrayed. I saw a direct correlation between each series—the first signified a range of ideals that pertained to the place itself, with the second referring more broadly to how residents might live (by representing more personalised attributes connected to lifestyle). This was a more confident, self-assured series of billboards that moved attention away from the development itself to display the type of people who live in Springfield Lakes. While the attributes of the first series are always in the background, we don't see explicit mention of Greater Springfield's *special places*, or choice of housing or belonging to the community. Those things are now presented as foundational characteristics of the development—assumed features that are now established and collectively understood—to the more personal identity characteristics individuals in Greater Springfield possess. A turn away from describing the place to a description of its residents is in play in this series.

These themes are certainly conflated in the supporting artifacts that correspond to these billboards. Use of the thematics deployed in these billboards extended into much of the marketing material to present a more complete picture of what residents *are* in Springfield Lakes. A key example of this includes a Delfin Springfield Lakes *Catch Up* Magazine from Autumn 2007 (Figure 32).

Using the imagery from the title billboard of the series (the young girl playing with bubbles), and the 'Catch Up' and 'Find Your Uplifting Place' slogans, this magazine functioned both as a community newsletter and sales brochure for houses in the area. The idea of 'catching up' takes on a slightly different meaning here, whereby it is the corporation catching up via the mechanism of a community newsletter that is significant. This is similar to the neighbourly feel the Orion Shopping Centre brochure suggested when it wished residents a 'Merry Christmas' from their 'newest neighbour'.

Again, the idea of a corporation functioning as an individual (or at least assuming a friendly identity) and wanting to 'catch up' is interesting and suggests something about the intention the *Springfield Land Corporation* and *Delfin* have to invest the development with a sense of interpersonal connectedness. As a brochure containing general interest articles about the latest stages of construction in the Springfield Lakes' development, and via labelling as the 'Catch Up', it almost substitutes for an informal morning tea between neighbours. Just as neighbours might get together and *catch up* about points of interest that are common to their neighbourhood, I can imagine this brochure being read by a resident sitting back with coffee, catching up with what is going on. Here, the ever-present Delfin and Springfield Land Corporation take on the role of being invited guests in your home; in this case, they do it in the form of a brochure.

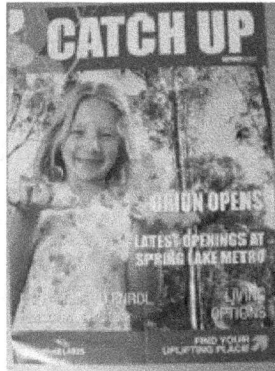

Figure 32: Catch Up magazine cover. Photo: Andrew Hickey.

In many ways the brochures, flyers and other artifacts that drew on the imagery and thematics of the billboards added meaning that the billboards (due to their restrictions of text and time scale passing motorists had to absorb their message) couldn't carry alone. Just as the '*What a Refreshing Change*' series of street banners were supported by flyers, magazines and brochures, artifacts such as the *Catch Up* magazine, and less prominently, the Delfin *Living Options* series of brochures provided context to the '*Find Your Uplifting Place*' series of billboards. Ultimately, a rich amalgam of meaning was generated through these inter-supporting artifacts.

The Brookwater Development

I move now out of *Springfield Lakes* and into the *Brookwater* sub-development within Greater Springfield. Billed as an exclusive golf-course development, the three series of billboards attached to Brookwater immediately suggested ideas of *distinction*—as Bourdieu (1987) would see it—masqueraded as a prestige and desire for 'the best'. I saw this manifestation of distinction as an elitism that was grounded in very specific determinants; firstly, an economic determinant attached to house and land prices, and secondly via a concern for style.

If Compromise Is Not in Your Nature

These billboards appeared along *Augusta Parkway*, the main connecting roadway between Springfield Lakes and Brookwater. As with the banners and signs of Springfield Lakes, the themes contained within these billboards were also utilised in other artifacts; primarily the *Brookwater News* community newsletter. The two billboards of this series follow similar formatting conventions to those deployed in the '*What a Refreshing Change*' series from Springfield Lakes; dominant imagery with supporting authorising words set around the perimeter of the billboard to contextualize the image and conflate the intended meaning of the Brookwater development.

Two very different subjects are the focus of the images captured in the billboards. The first presents a jazz band fronted by a female singer (Figure 33), with the second showing an open-plan living and dining space in one of Brookwater's 'gallery' homes (Figure 34). A suggestion of refined elegance is common to both—here the application of distinction as an 'aesthetic disposition' (Bourdieu 1987: 261) is ever present (the jazz band is dressed elegantly in tuxedos and exudes a reserved 'cool' whilst the open plan design and tasteful furnishings of the gallery home express a sophistication and refinement). In these images 'compromising' isn't an option; the Brookwater resident is someone who only settles for the best, a person who appreciates quality, style, sophistication and elegance, and it is those things displayed by the image that signify what the 'best' is.

In terms of format, the viewer takes the position of outsider looking in— the viewpoint is cast from outside the image into the physical spaces of Brookwater's homes and leisure venues. But unlike Springfield Lakes, the suggestion of the people of Brookwater is left vague; while we might make guesses at who lives in Brookwater based on how they've decorated the part of their vacant home viewed in the second billboard, or by their taste in music noted in the first, no representatives of Brookwater are presented to base our assumptions. There just aren't any people from Brookwater positioned within the billboards to give us a human connection to life in Brookwater (I've assumed of course that the jazz band members aren't residents but hired entertainers for the residents' amusement).

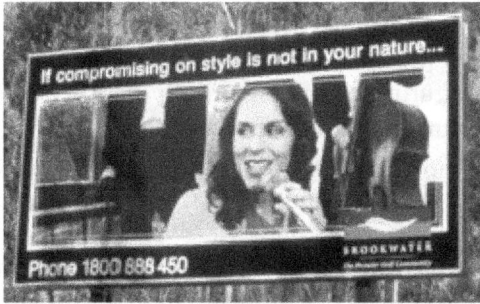

Figure 33: Brookwater's 'jazz' distinction. Photo: Andrew Hickey.

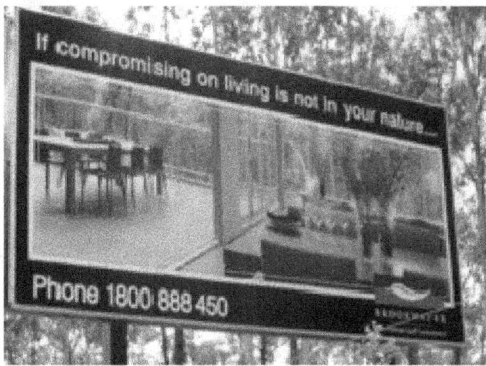

Figure 34: Compromise isn't an option. Photo: Andrew Hickey.

This is significantly different to the billboards of Springfield Lakes where we see residents engaged in activities within its physical spaces to become prime components of the marketing of the space. In Brookwater, the viewer of the billboards is left to guess what sorts of people live here and how they go about leading their uncompromising lifestyles.

The thing that struck me with these billboards was precisely these features—the lack of people, and the suggestion of distinction. It is also these factors that make the Brookwater experience as viewed in these billboards austerely individualistic. Unlike the Springfield Lakes celebration of its residents and the relaxed, comfortable lifestyle these people are shown to lead, Brookwater is represented as being far more absent, detached and exacting. Are these absent residents too busy in their corporate lives to be at home whiling away hours of comfortable leisure? Or are they indeed playing golf on the neighbouring course from which the development gets its name and reputation? Either way, people are missing and this says something about this place, particularly when compared to the resident-rich imagery of Springfield Lakes.

In terms of the jazz band billboard, I have imagined there to be a genteel cocktail party occurring outside of the framed boundaries of the image. This speculation might be furthered by suggesting that this is perhaps the sort of belonging and community that residents express in Brookwater. There isn't any need to overlook a park for the kids (you are, by virtue of the house prices, most likely a double income, no kids 'power couple') or to get the neighbours over for a barbeque (*a* barbeque—how suburban!). In Brookwater, getting together is altogether more formal, refined and sophisticated. It has jazz as entertainment, and locations like *Armstrong's at Brookwater* for dining. It is about style and 'prestige addresses' that 'reflect the buyer's position in life' (The Big Picture *Health Special*, November-December 2006). In this sense Brookwater represents *exclusivity*:

> Brookwater has officially launched its ultimate address, Augusta Point. With gated access and bounded by three fairways, Augusta Point is nothing short of being truly private and exclusive, with latest sales reaching $525,000…. Augusta Point will offer access control and no through traffic, making it one of the most anticipated prestige land releases in the region. Brookwater resident architect, Stephen Drake, said the large level home sites would be conducive to homes and gardens worthy of the address. (Big Picture *Health Special*, November-December, 2006)

As represented by *Augusta Point* (Brookwater's 'ultimate address'), residents don't need to worry about the riff-raff from neighbouring (and socio-economically depressed) suburbs coming to vandalise property; this is a gated community with 'access control'. Residents don't simply 'build' a home in Brookwater; they choose from architecturally designed 'addresses'. They similarly don't have to put up with second best in the aesthetics of the peripherals of the home; the gardens and space to grow these are 'worthy'.

It is exclusivity as a recurring keyword in many of the artifacts attached to Brookwater that specifically signifies the type of distinction present in Brookwater. Exclusivity carries with it the logic of the two determinants of distinction I noted above; exclusivity is cast in terms of the pre-requisite economic 'position' its residents require in order to be able to live here, but it also reflects an 'exclusive aesthetic' that presents as a concern for and understanding of the style that living in such a surround requires. I argue that what is being suggested here is a *reserved privatism* that captures the concerns of a competitive consumerist logic and individualism all at once. To be in Brookwater means being 'successful' economically and understanding how economic systems operate. But it also requires an understanding of how this success should be expressed—primarily via the houses and lifestyle of places like Augusta Point. At the same time, this logic is conflated by a privatism that doesn't give any indication as to the 'inside' world of residents. These are people who can command privacy and reservation. That only a glimpse of the inside life of a Brookwater home was offered in the second billboard says much on this—I almost had the feeling that this billboard provided permission for me to take a glimpse of what was on offer inside Brookwater (in some ways like a property inspection hosted by an estate agent). This privatism when contrasted against the celebration of residents in Springfield Lakes certainly said something about the private nature of inside life at Brookwater—it is far more exclusive than the 'community' oriented Springfield Lakes.

Because...

A second series of billboards advertising Brookwater appeared soon after those positioned on Augusta Parkway. This series followed a similar logic to the first two billboards (and explicitly continued the 'compromise' theme in one of its billboards). Imagery in these billboards was less prominent with authorising words assuming a far greater significance than in any of the other billboards located in Greater Springfield at this time. Identified via the recurring 'Because' keyword, these banners suggested reasons for selecting Brookwater as a place to live, and offered prospective residents an idea about what to expect—primarily:

1. inspiration from beauty in the form of a flower in bloom (Figure 35),
2. a lifestyle selected after a considered life change (Figure 37), and
3. a discernment displayed as an unwillingness to compromise, visualised by a resident clipping a single out-of-place blade of grass with scissors (Figure 36).

At the same time that personal agency is suggested by this series (principally via the ability prospective residents have to rethink their lives and move to Brookwater), a significant uniformity is visualised via the lone, renegade blade of grass being clipped back into compliance in Figure 36. Just as with the first series of Brookwater billboards, residents here don't compromise, they aspire to perfection represented by such things as uniformly manicured lawns, and the appreciation of aesthetic beauty in the form of Brookwater's gardens (as signified by the flower in the first billboard). This is a series of billboards that carries the sense of reserved privatism of the first, but fills in the picture a little more by giving an indication about how residents express this; namely via their uncompromising nature. These are not so much advertisements for the Brookwater development, but suggestions to prospective residents about their status and eligibility to become part of the place.

Figure 35: Because–inspired by beauty. Photo: Andrew Hickey.

Figure 36: Because–compromise is not in your nature. Photo: Andrew Hickey.

Figure 37: Rethink your life at Brookwater. Photo: Andrew Hickey.

The location of the Brookwater billboards was also remarkable. The largest of the three (noting the '*Because its time to rethink the way you live*' slogan) was displayed along the *Western Arterial Road* leading into

Springfield Lakes from the *Centenary Highway* (the major highway into Greater Springfield). This billboard was later accompanied by two further billboards that contained the short catch phrases 'Be Indulgent. Have Everything' (as viewed on the entry into Springfield Lakes) and 'Drive through beautiful countryside every weekend' (on the way from Springfield Lakes heading west towards the *Centenary Highway*). Simple black text overlaid on a white background was all these billboards contained (with a small 'Brookwater' logo listed under the text).

I found it fascinating that these signs were located at a relative distance from Brookwater itself (by comparison, the other billboards in these series were both located along the *Augusta Parkway* thoroughfare in Brookwater). I suggest that these signs assumed two purposes; of course, they operated as marketing devices and suggested something about the development and its characteristics. But secondly, and due to their location, these billboards symbolically fulfilled the role of reminding users of the busy *Western Arterial* about Brookwater. These were signs that said something about residents of Brookwater to all who passed (they affirmed Brookwater residents' unwillingness to accept compromise, assert their distinction and enjoy indulgence). These signs reminded other Greater Springfield residents that Brookwater was different; these towering signifiers told travellers of the *Western Arterial* something quite specific about what Brookwater was, even before they had entered the place.

—Conflating the Banners

Quite overt sanctions were deployed in the billboards of Brookwater when considered in terms of the sheer economic determinants required to live there. But combined with these, implicit suggestions of style and distinction worked to form a very specific rationale upon which residents were 'measured'. As with the suggestions deployed by the banners and artifacts of Springfield Lakes, living in Brookwater wasn't simply about having enough money to buy a house. The suggestions drawn from the billboards also said much about how residents should lead their lives, and what sorts of 'style' they should follow. A very prescriptive mode of living was suggested; one that merges with wider themes of urban decay, the protection of private property and maintenance of personal safety to result in a development that is lauded in terms of its secure 'gated' nature, concern for the maintenance of aesthetics and 'private' space. This logic even extended in the early billboards to the space of the private home. In none of the imagery deployed in the various magazines, brochures and other artifacts advertising Brookwater did I see anyone other than the presumed owners of the residence being displayed (if indeed people were displayed at all—to even see the owners of the residence in advertisements was rare). Inside space in Brookwater was a sanctuary—that prize successful people who didn't compromise were rewarded with. This subsequently resulted in an almost *lonely* individualism where people, gated securely in the enclave of their exclusive residences, indulged in life (albeit, on their own).

As with Springfield Lakes, a range of glossy mail-out newsletters and pamphlets to residents was disseminated in Brookwater. Most prominent amongst these was the *Brookwater News* (Figure 38), a large glossy community newsletter distributed from early 2007 that contained general interest editorials about the development and house sales advertisements. While it followed many of the formatting principles as the *Springfield Lakes Community Update* (it was A3 sized, glossy and contained a mixture of general interest editorials about the area and property advertisements— Figure 39), it utilised a more formally typeset banner. I read this as fitting with the austere nature of Brookwater as presented through its billboards. While the script utilised in the *Springfield Lakes Community Update* suggested an informal, 'carefree' feel, the *Brookwater News* contrasted markedly. The other feature of these semiotic characteristics is the differentiation in purpose for each artifact—in Brookwater residents are provided with 'news', whilst in Springfield Lakes an 'update' is what is disseminated. Again, this carries with it the logic of the billboards presented in each location—in Springfield Lakes a relaxed sense of belonging is suggested, whilst in Brookwater far more reserved austerity is presented.

Building on the theme of distinction that permeated the billboards of Brookwater, artifacts such as the *Brookwater News* and those various other brochures and flyers maintained the sense of exclusivity as a hallmark feature of the place. A key example of this conflation of exclusivity across the various artifacts is demonstrated by a brochure advertising 'The Grange'—an 'exclusive gated precinct'—located alongside the Brookwater Golf Course:

> The Grange is an exclusive gated precinct of just 50 luxury villas set discretely within the master planned community of prestigious Brookwater. Privacy and a sense of community are the key concepts at The Grange, with many villas enjoying views over Brookwater's magnificent golf course and the natural bushland setting. All aspects of a low maintenance, comfortable lifestyle have been considered in the design of The Grange, from the entry statement and manicured landscaping to the villa designs on individual lots.
> (*The Grange: Resort Living at Brookwater* flyer, 2007)

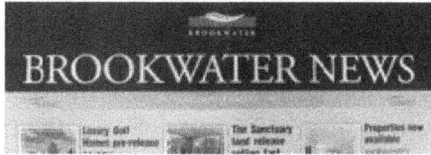

Figure 38: Brookwater News banner head. Photo: Andrew Hickey.

Figure 39: Springfield Lakes Community Update banner head. Photo: Andrew Hickey.

Exclusivity-as-distinction manifested in the form of the finer aspects of lifestyle in Brookwater. Things such as the appointment of an executive chef at the premier, fine-dining restaurant in the *Brookwater Clubhouse* and mention of the prestige of residences available in Brookwater feature in the artifacts as descriptors of Brookwater's distinction:

> Only twenty-one prestige residences will be part of Augusta Point, eighteen of which will offer stunning, uninterrupted views of the golf course; making it one of the most beautiful locations on offer in today's residential marketplace... This address is of a premium and will continue to be Brookwater's best for years to come. (*Brookwater News*, January–February 2007, advertising the Augusta Point development)

The artifacts I collected during my time in Greater Springfield suggested much about the desire the developers of Brookwater had to demarcate the development as exclusive. Exclusivity followed as a reserved privatism in the artifacts as it did in the billboards, where an individualistic sense of distinction defined against determinants of economic wealth and style mediated the identity characteristics residents were represented as having. Just as in Springfield Lakes, where family, belonging, opportunity and education featured as hallmark characteristics the ideal resident should possess, Brookwater too contained its own set of identity markers for residents. But in this case, they were far more tied to senses of distinction and exclusivity.

Other Signs in Greater Springfield

Apart from the billboards and those brochures, flyers and other artifacts collected during my time in Greater Springfield, the development also contained a range of signs that variously suggested the logic of the space and gave an indication of phenomena such as community decay (I explore this below). These variously formal and informal, sanctioned and unsanctioned signs all added to the readings of Greater Springfield derived from those billboards and other artifacts explored above and provided further understandings of what this development *meant*. Some of the more significant signs displayed in Greater Springfield include the following.

Graffiti and Informal Signs

Responsibility for the production of signs wasn't limited to the developers alone. A number of other authorised and not-so-authorised signs also appeared during my time there. Varying from flyers advertising church services to brochures left under the windscreen wipers of cars, Greater Springfield was no different from any other social milieu in that it contained a plethora of signs signifying services, public announcements, advertisements and other information sources.

One source of signage that I was particularly drawn to however was graffiti.[10] Graffiti became noticeable largely due to its absence[11] in Springfield Lakes and Brookwater, and appeared primarily in 'old' Springfield; the original development of Greater Springfield located to the north of Springfield Lakes. The only evidence I had of graffiti in Springfield Lakes was a collection of very basic 'tags' and similar scrawl overlaid on a sign describing the biodiversity of its artificial lakes. Apart from this, graffiti as a form of informal and potentially resistant communication resided in old Springfield. This isn't to suggest that the amount of graffiti was in any way prolific or its style elaborate or aesthetically sophisticated. In general, graffiti in Springfield consisted of basic 'tags' and other symbolic signifiers of the artist's identity and presence.

I suggest that the lack of graffiti in Springfield Lakes and Brookwater—the more contemporary and affluent ends of the Greater Springfield development—was largely due to three causes:

---

[10] I suggest that this form of signage was 'graffiti' as opposed to 'street art'. The definition I apply here sees street art as far more elaborate aesthetically and as a form of communication that contains an intentioned artistic characteristic. Graffiti, such as that seen in Springfield were basic scrawls and tags and didn't contain elaborate artistic intent. As such, I use the term *graffiti* to describe such signage.

[11] This is remarkable, as Brisbane and Ipswich have well-known street art scenes. *Stencil Revolution* (2008) notes a 2004 competition between Melbourne and Brisbane based street artists that identified a thriving street art sub-culture in Brisbane. This sub-culture as yet hasn't permeated Greater Springfield.

1. the newness and subsequent 'protection' of these areas by the developers through security services,
2. the privatized contract maintenance services that existed to keep the parks and public spaces looking pristine, and
3. the general gentrification of these areas that meant that teenagers, as that demographic of people most closely attributed as graffiti artists, didn't live within them (Springfield Lakes has a 'young family' demographic, whilst Brookwater tends to be populated with childless couples).

A local police constable suggested that graffiti was becoming an issue in Greater Springfield's older sections; he had speculated that this was due to young people from the less affluent neighbouring suburbs of *Camira*, *Inala* and *Goodna* coming *into* (he certainly saw this as an outside threat) old Springfield at night to 'vandalise property' (Corey, 12th November 2007). This speculation about vandals from outside Springfield entering the area was also repeated by several of my other informants, and added to a theme of self-identification in Greater Springfield; an 'us' constituted by residents of Greater Springfield and a 'them' constituted by people living in the less affluent surrounding suburbs.

But in all, the graffiti of Greater Springfield was, for a major urban space, minimal and didn't signify to any real extent the presence of organised groupings of people; that is, gangs of graffiti artists. It didn't surprise me to see the most elaborate graffiti located on a skateboard park (the only public space that I could see was dedicated to teenagers in Greater Springfield—Figure 40) and a dimly lit billboard located in old Springfield (it was almost asking for trouble to place a billboard in a quiet, poorly lit end of town!). Apart from this, graffiti didn't maintain the significance as a form of unauthorised and resistant public signage that I expected this large urban space to contain. Again, I can only assume that those features I suggested above (the 'newness', security regime and gentrification of the area) resulted in only those older and peripheral 'outer' edges of Greater Springfield being targeted.

The Decay of Old Springfield

My observation of graffiti in old Springfield led me to look a little more closely at the decay that had set in to the original Greater Springfield development. Driving out of Springfield Lakes, up *Springfield Parkway* and over the hill to old Springfield, I noticed a real sense of difference between the 'feel' of the two suburbs. It was almost as if the hill between the Lakes and old Springfield presented as a geographic boundary across which one travelled to see what Springfield Lakes *wasn't*. I noticed that the contract maintenance services didn't go into old Springfield[12] and that its lawns were long, parks overgrown and that things just looked a bit 'old' by comparison.

Figure 40: Graffiti and the skate park. Photo: Andrew Hickey.

Symbolically, this was summed up for me by the state of ruin to which the landmark 'Springfield' (Figure 41) sign had fallen into by the time I completed my fieldwork in Greater Springfield. When I first arrived, the sign was largely intact, albeit missing segments of lettering. Two years later, the missing lettering had been repaired, but graffiti tags had also been added (I assume from different sign-writers). A year after this, the western end of the sign had been pushed over; it remained this way up to the time I completed my fieldwork.

I found it entirely remarkable that this sign—this symbolic signifier of the pride that attached to the first development in Greater Springfield—could be left in such a state of disrepair. This was the sign I saw proudly displayed in marketing materials for the early Springfield development; a sign that stood for the freshness and dynamism of this place. But akin to Shelley's *Ozymandias*, it now represented the decay of the older end of Greater Springfield. The Lakes were now the symbol of Greater Springfield's essence, and that's where the attentions of the developers had shifted.

---

[12] I saw this specifically on one fieldtrip where the contractors mowing the lawn stopped mowing literally on the edge of the rise that symbolically demarcated the end of the Lakes and the start of old Springfield. The short, manicured lawns of the Lakes and the long, overgrown lawns of old Springfield from that point on represented for me the nature of the difference between the two places.

Figure 41: Symbolic decay. Photo: Andrew Hickey

What the Signs Said

The significance of signs in Greater Springfield cannot be overstated. Whether in the form of billboards or brochures, these composites of imagery and catch phrases provided a prescribed image of what life in Greater Springfield could be. Naturally, these signs were deployed as marketing tools and were designed to be idealistic, but it was the broad parameters from which they presented their ideals that suggested something about what Greater Springfield not only *could* be, but in fact had turned out *to* be. From the paleosymbolic ideals these signs suggested developed an indication of the logic of Greater Springfield—a collective epistemological creation of meaning upon which the place came to be understood and experienced.

I focused heavily in this chapter on the signs of Springfield Lakes, Brookwater and to a lesser extent (old) Springfield. There were other developments within Greater Springfield, such as *Augustine Heights* and *Brentwood* that similarly also deployed a range of signs explaining what these developments *were*. But it was the frequency and completeness of the suggestions presented by the signs in Springfield Lakes and Brookwater that stood out as significant.[13] As much as these physical spaces of the development were pre-formed and made ready for residents, suggestions on how to live within them (presented symbolically via signage) were similarly ready for consumption. A guidebook on how to live was presented by the signs of Greater Springfield.

The importance of these signs was their everyday-ness. These mundane, ubiquitous objects of the development became significant indicators of the place for this reason. These things were everywhere, and while the

---

[13] This is perhaps not surprising, as both developments were the major developments of this space.

suggestions for lifestyle that they carried were a bit spectacular, their ubiquity made them a largely accepted part of the landscape. No one I spoke with in Greater Springfield saw anything extraordinary about the presence of these signs. They were a part of Greater Springfield, but a part that carried significance (as I saw it) due to the ability they had to actively present certain views of living and lifestyle.

Making Sense of the Signs

I now turn my attention from what the idealised images of Springfield life contained in the billboards, banners, brochures and other artifacts suggested to asking what life in Greater Springfield was like from the perspective of those who lived there. *Chapter 4* presents the ideas of those people attached to Greater Springfield and explores what this place meant to them, but to finish this chapter and to offer one last reading of the signs of Greater Springfield, I want to look at one last quote from a Delfin brochure distributed in Springfield Lakes:

> At Delfin Living Options Springfield Lakes, there's something to suit every budget and lifestyle. (Delfin *Summer Living* Magazine, November 2006)

The suggestion here is that there is something for everyone at Springfield Lakes. Of course, this is good marketing practice; by suggesting that a range of choice is available, a wider market of potential investors is opened. But it isn't all that accurate a suggestion. There isn't in fact a lot of actual choice available, and what is available is presented in terms of a couple of variations of brick-veneer detached housing, familiar styles of retail outlets and parkland that functions as parkland does in most other parts of Australia (albeit in a contemporary, landscaped with native flora, kind of way). While subtle differences in terms of an overriding 'philosophy' exist (expressed by a specific style of aesthetic and finish), the Greater Springfield developments are still just urban developments that, in this case, cater to an affluent middle-class market. Very specific (and as I will suggest in *Chapter 5*, 'traditional') identity characteristics pertain to the desired inhabitants of Greater Springfield. There is nothing in the design and construction that suggests anything other than an archetypal Western, middle-class existence.

And this is exactly the rub. There is no such thing as the '*archetypal Western, middle-class existence*' apart from that which exists in the idealised imagery of the billboards of places like Greater Springfield. This is the style of living that is created as much as it is catered to, and more significantly, where the image is maintained as a point of aspiration. To 'suit' you, as the Delfin brochure suggests, Greater Springfield has catered to every possible need, price range and desire. But we know that this is in fact impossible—no development constructed from a single vision and philosophy could ever hope to achieve something for everyone. So what is left is the pretence of inclusion that in fact presents a desirable life ethic that by its very nature excludes everything that isn't presented in the image. Here is a place that exists because of its imagery and maintains its imagery via its physicality (I recall the point made earlier in this chapter that it is actual residents who are drawn on to feature in advertising for Springfield Lakes; here, *the real maintains the image*). This place is a simulacrum (Baudrillard 1994) that is modelled off the imagery of its own creation.

The idea of community is strangely protected by this logic. As an expression of collective interaction and similarity (a shared sense of being in the world), community, as it is presented by the signs of Greater Springfield, translates an image of comfortable affluence, relaxed leisure, the enjoyment of open space, the belonging of family and friends and a sense of distinction. But this is a contrived sense of community; one that is mediated in the first instance by the desires of the developers and presented via the billboards and signs distributed in the place to appeal to people who similarly find the place appealing enough to fit in with its pre-fabricated logic. This is not an organic community expressed as a mutually formed sense of collective interaction, but an amalgam of folks who have the money, sense of style and approach to lifestyle that fit with what the development has become. This is a community of a sale demographic manufactured through the power of signage.

Now, what do the residents have to say about this?

Chapter 4

Living with Signs: Community, Individualism and Urban Space

All of it's a myth. A lot of mythology surrounds what Springfield and Springfield Lakes are and often doesn't reflect the reality.

—Rebecca, *Greater Springfield Resident*

I know what you mean when you say it is a strange place because it doesn't make sense. But a whole heap of people seem to think it must…because they choose to live here.

—Louise, *Greater Springfield Resident*

I was amazed with how the lofty idealism presented by the authorised signs of the developments of Greater Springfield compared to everyday facets of living. It wasn't that the ideals presented by the billboards were wrong, or worse, intentionally misleading, but that they captured a very specific view of what life *could* be like. This after all was a community of several thousand people, with perhaps as many interpretations of 'the vision' as there were people residing in Greater Springfield. While the images and suggestions for living presented by the signs of Greater Springfield represented an *imagined* (Anderson 1983) form of community connectedness and self-identification, the ideals the signs contained were something that I found residents didn't automatically accept in their 'real' day-to-day lives.

Naturally, the point of advertising media, such as those billboards and brochures I looked at in the previous chapter, is to sell an image of what something could be—this is the 'desire' that Hebdidge notes in his application of Delueze and Guatari's idea of the 'desiring machine':

Advertising provides an endless succession of vacatable positions for the 'desiring machines'. (Hebdidge 1988:211)

The billboards and brochures showed what could be done—or perhaps more correctly, what *should* be done in Greater Springfield as intended by its developers. But living in Greater Springfield wasn't simply a process of residents seeing, wanting and becoming. The 'desiring machines' of Greater Springfield—its residents—had their own agency and ideas about what life should be like and didn't always fall for the imagery to blandly re-create what they saw. In fact, disregard and active criticism of the images was presented by several of those people I spent time with; one in particular noted that the idealism of the imagery was 'a load of rubbish, to be quite honest' (Jane, 12th November 2007).

What occurred to me was that the imagery of Greater Springfield didn't function along a basis of a simple dialectic; a dualism where the ideals of Greater Springfield's signage sat in one corner, and the residents in the other. The imagery did exert a certain influence. It did set a logic for the place. It did define the boundary and how things came to be known in Greater Springfield. But the residents also presented their own views—alternative views in many cases—and actively critiqued how ideals of community and collective living were premised in the signage. As the intent of public pedagogies prescribes however, certain residents may have been critical of the idealistic imagery of the billboards and brochures, their criticisms were simultaneously bound by the very logic of the imagery itself. A complex relationship to the place emerged here, where Greater Springfieldians, whether for or against the ideals promulgated by Delfin and the Springfield Land Corporation, came to see themselves *as* or *not as* 'the sort of person who lives in Greater Springfield' (Jane, 12th November 2007).[1] Here was the public pedagogical implication for the signage. It didn't matter that residents agreed or disagreed, *but that they reacted to it* in one way or other. The very logic of the place was affirmed whether people agreed or not—the logic was already framed.

This was striking for me, because it suggested that my informants had a clear idea of what sort of person lived in Greater Springfield, and perhaps more implicitly, whether that 'sort of person' was the sort of person they were. Jane in particular seemed to battle the most with this—she was deeply critical of what Greater Springfield had become, and of how Delfin had constructed the place as a contrived form of community. She became impassioned and angry as she told me these things whilst she overlooked her young son playing on swings as I talked to her in a park. She particularly

---

[1]   Several of my other informants (Mike, Pete and Maree) also alluded to there being such a thing as the 'Springfield Lakes person', as if some sort of archetypal Springfield resident did exist.

noted how she felt isolated within this 'community' and had recently made the decision to move away:

Jane: ...I just don't like the whole 'community', kind of thing—imposed community. And I feel that it is an imposed community.

Andrew: And you find that you feel pressured to be part of the community when you might just want to be on your own?

Jane: Sometimes...Where we're living at the moment, we're kind of all piled on top of one another. I'm not really a community...kind of person, really.

Andrew: So who would it suit most here? Do you think there's a particular kind of person?

Jane: I just think people that are really into socialising and like that kind of whole community thing.

Andrew: So for folks who like their space, it's a bit too full on?

Jane: ...being on top of people. I find because you're so close together you've got no choice but to feel involved with people, even if you don't necessarily want to be. You can't really keep yourselves to yourselves. (Jane, 12th November 2007)

Jane was critical of the way that the ideals of Greater Springfield, presented via those same billboards and brochures I explored in the previous chapter, transcended the realm of the image alone to be representative of the entire logic of the place. While she indeed expressed a desire to have 'space' (geographic primarily, but I also took this to refer to a conceptual space) to exert her agency and live how she desired, she noted that there was still a pressure—albeit perhaps as an implicitly self-assumed pressure—to be involved in something she didn't connect with. Ultimately, the ideals of life in Greater Springfield as expressed by the artifacts and witnessed by her experiences of life in Greater Springfield didn't meet her needs, and as such she had decided to leave.[2]

My key informant Rebecca noted that while she could see what Delfin and the Springfield Land Corporation were attempting to achieve with the imagery of life in Greater Springfield, she questioned the intent behind the application of it:

I think when Delfin discuss community it's certainly a marketing spin, absolutely. But then on the other hand they have put up community groups that don't make a profit for them—but I suppose the fringe benefit of that would be that it might attract people to move into the community and keep it vibrant and so forth. So yeah, I don't buy into their version of community whatsoever.

---

[2] Moving later that month, as it turned out, to a development close by that offered larger block sizes and a more 'rural aspect'.

> However…Springfield is a community—it's a community because people
> live there and people work there and play there and their children are there.
> So I think even despite some cheesy commercials and cheesy marketing, a
> community will develop anyway. Because people are people…and they want
> to have interactions with other humans. (Rebecca, 7th November 2007)

Talking in terms of the way that community manifested in Greater
Springfield, Rebecca, a long-term resident and local educator[3], suggested that
residents interacted regardless of the ideals presented by the developers of
the place. Like anywhere, she argued, people would get together and do
things as they needed and how they needed.

This was the nature of the views of Greater Springfield. While the
imagery presented by the signs suggested an idealised view of how life in
Greater Springfield functioned, the residents exerted and lived their own
views of things within the structural constraints of the development (such as
its sheer physicality and logic). The underpinning logic of the development
as mediated by the developers was ever-present; the way the built
environment was structured, the nature of the type of housing available, the
services provided and the expectations for maintaining the financial
investment of owning a part of Greater Springfield were undeniable and
suggested more than what the physicality of the place superficially presented.
But outside of the social expectations of these constraints and amongst the
suggestions for living presented by the signage developed an agency from
which residents appropriated what was pre-formed in the built environment
to meet the demands of what they wanted.

But, as Schutzman suggests, flows of advertising as information
dissemination devices present a peculiar dilemma in the late-capitalist world:

> We desiring machines roam haphazardly in ad-inspired fugue states, ever
> shopping, seeking self-improvement and satisfaction. When we fail, as we
> always do, we try again… But in our search for happiness, commodities
> deliver us to the pearly gates short-sighted and impotent. Our ephemeral
> dreams were masterfully packaged in things that leave us only smoke and
> mirrors, just as the profiteers intended it. (1999: 118)

In Jane's case, themes of 'self-improvement and satisfaction' presented by
the 'Find Your Uplifting Place' series of billboards, for instance, didn't
respond to her desire, to the point that she felt pathologised in the
'claustrophobic' and 'imposed community' (Jane, 12th November 2007) of
Greater Springfield:

---

[3] Rebecca had worked for several years as a teacher in one of the high schools in Greater
Springfield.

| Andrew: | So what is the moral of the story if one was contemplating moving to Springfield...? |
| Jane: | Don't move to a community if you don't want to be a community person. As much as they try to be inclusive, it can be exclusive. (Jane, 12th November 2007) |

The glossy images of belonging, community, lifestyle and connectedness didn't quite translate for Jane. Greater Springfield for her had become a very isolating experience—an experience that fitted a certain *type* of person (as she noted, a 'community person'). While choices could be made within the pre-formed environments of Greater Springfield and appropriations of its logic deployed, it remained that a boundary of agency functioned to authorise specific identity claims and modes of living. As Rebecca noted, while it may well have been possible for residents to deride the imagery of Greater Springfield as marketing spin, it still did maintain a benchmark upon which modes of lifestyle were intended and upon which the entire physicality of Greater Springfield—its buildings, parklands and shopping centres—was constructed. It was from this that its logic flowed. To live in Greater Springfield meant, at least in part, accepting a certain understanding about who you were as measured against who the ideal Greater Springfield resident was. The signs of Greater Springfield provided clear visual cues as to what this was. The built environment, configuration of public space and nature of the services available in the place further mediated the style of living and type of person the Greater Springfield resident *should* be.

Critiquing the Image

One significant theme that emerged from talking with residents and by simply being in Greater Springfield was that while the imagery of Greater Springfield was widely criticised for its idealism, it was simultaneously considered to be the basis of what Greater Springfield *was*. My informants derided the billboards and brochures at the same time as they drew on the same themes suggested in them. They didn't do this directly—that is, by referring to a specific billboard image and saying '*there, that is what Greater Springfield is like*'. But they did repeat the themes captured by the imagery and utilise specific terms like 'belonging', 'choice' and 'community' to describe the place as they spoke with me. I took this as being further expression of the pre-framed logic of Greater Springfield. These meta-narratives and the idealism they carried via signage demonstrated the effects of the public pedagogical processes attached to Greater Springfield's identity manufacturing. This was the basis upon which the logic of Greater Springfield was formed.

Jane's suggestion that you had to be a certain type of person to reside in Greater Springfield resonated with me. Rebecca as well had inferred in several of the meetings I had with her that there were specific types of people encouraged in Greater Springfield, even though she suggested that *other* types of people lived and worked within it. As a long-term resident of Greater Springfield, Rebecca noted that the development had notable populations of people from the Pacifika region and from Southeast Asia; but these faces didn't show in any of the billboards or brochures. My own observations also suggested that types of people *I didn't see* presented in the billboards and brochures called Greater Springfield home; alternatives to the white, heterosexual, upwardly mobile identities suggested in the imagery did exist in Greater Springfield, even though its signage didn't suggest so.

Even segments of the same media sources that carried expressions of the Springfield Land Corporation and Delfin vision offered an alternative perspective of what life in Greater Springfield was like. One striking example included John Walker's report from the *Sunday Mail* newspaper's 'Q Weekend' supplement:

> I met 17-year-old mechanic Doug Wilson and his mates, Robbie Whittaker and Andrew Nelson, at the front of Wilson's home on Orchid Place. I asked Wilson what he thought of Sinnathamby's vision. 'I don't know who you are talking about,' he said. I explained: community, family, cradle-to-grave. Whittaker laughed out loud. Wilson laughed with him. 'I'll be here for another four years, max, and I'll be gone,' Wilson said. 'There's nothing here' Whittaker said. 'Nothing, it's a place for retirement'. 'At night it gets violent', Wilson said.
> Mother of five Deborah Van Bennekom has seen a 'whole new generation of youth' emerge in Springfield. The children who came with their young parents in the mid-90s are now teenagers. And they haven't it seems fitted snugly into the masterplan.
> I went back to the creator. I asked him about the future for Springfield's youth. 'My form of entertainment for children is to take part in study and take part in sport' said Sinnathamby... 'Any entertainment, like a city life, we don't have that. Quite honestly, we are trying to create a society that is highly motivated, highly concerned about education and highly concerned about sport'.
> The vision is splendid. The reality, however, is clouded in dust.
> 'A builder mate of mine said they had to change the plan of the homes because you couldn't get the wheelie bin around the hot-water system to put it out front'. (Walker October 7–8 2006:21)

Alternative visions such as this stood in contrast to the carefully marketed imagery of the artifacts I explored in the previous chapter. What emerged from the accounts I captured of the Greater Springfield experience was a binary or dualism that contained at each of its ends the 'image and the real' (Hickey and Austin 2006). In the case of Walker's story and the vision expressed by the artifacts explored in the previous chapter, some residents' *real* experiences stood as something significantly different from those mediated experiences displayed in the imagery. The thing I wanted to know, was how different it was and how they felt about this. In the efforts the developers made to market towards a specific demographic and market segment, what remained were alternative views about Greater Springfield that weren't being captured in the authorised and dominant visions of the place. Jane's experience in particular stood as a key example of this— specifically as she now felt she could no longer stay in Greater Springfield because of it.

The Ideas of the Residents

My informants came from a range of backgrounds and walks of life. Essentially, they fitted into one of three categories: i. Rebecca my key informant, ii. representatives from The Springfield Land Corporation, Delfin and other development companies in Greater Springfield and iii. residents and others associated with Greater Springfield. While many more interviews and discussions were conducted than could be reported here, what follows are the accounts from informants who articulated representative views about what they felt Greater Springfield *meant*.

I saw six major themes emerge from my discussions with my informants. Ideas about what community *is* in Greater Springfield followed from questions I asked concerning the nature and identity of its community. This led into discussions about the nature of a 'Greater Springfield identity' and who it was that called this place home. From these discussions some of my informants suggested that ideas of wealth, affluence and exclusivity stood as key markers of who people were in Greater Springfield. These themes suggested an awareness of a specific cultural capital in the development; one central to expressions of lifestyle. From here, some informants suggested that the imagery of life in Greater Springfield suggested by signage produced a self-fulfilling logic—that intending residents *became* residents due to their willingness to accept what was offered and set about living their lives according to the types of lifestyle afforded in Greater Springfield. This theme directly suggested the operation of a public pedagogy that asserted a set of identity characteristics over Greater Springfield and its residents. Finally, a phenomenon titled the '*the Delfin effect*', as noted by two of my informants (Louise and Rebecca), emerged as a significant theme in our discussions. The Delfin effect referred to an insularity that these informants suggested had formed in Greater Springfield due to the well-used slogan that Greater Springfield is a place 'where [residents] can work, live and play all within the one community' (Nicole, 28th March 2007).

 I present my analysis of my informants' thoughts and ideas according to these six themes collated in the sections that follow.

Community and the Greater Springfield Resident

The idea of community was an important one in the discussions I had with my informants. While I did ask my informants directly what they thought community meant in Greater Springfield, it regularly appeared as a key concept in the conceptualisations and descriptions they offered of Greater Springfield. The complexity of the term and my informants' definitions meant that I captured a multifaceted view of what community came to mean, and as such, various sub-themes emerged to fill in the idea of community as it was held by my informants. Here are their descriptions.

What Is Community?

I generally opened discussions with my informants by asking them what they thought community meant in Greater Springfield. Early on in the interview stage of this project, I had arranged to meet with Nicole and Debbie, two representatives of Delfin who worked in the marketing section of the company:

Andrew:	In a nutshell could you tell me what community means to this place?
Debbie:	Sense of belonging.
Nicole:	Yes that's it in a nutshell, yes.
Debbie:	Sense of belonging.
Nicole:	That says it all I think. Sense of belonging which is what our job is, to try and foster within the community. So when people purchase in from a developers point of view when people purchase into our development that they're moving into somewhere where they can—
	I know it sounds like a catch-phrase but where they can work, live and play all within the one community. And we sort of help assist in the setup of social infrastructure within the community so that people feel like they actually belong here. (Nicole and Debbie, 28th March 2007)

Being part of Greater Springfield was an important aspect of community for Nicole and Debbie, and as part of their job, felt they had a key role in maintaining the connectedness of community. While I was sceptical early on in the interview that I was being fed the 'company line'—that Nicole and Debbie were simply repeating what their marketing department required its staff to say about the development—I came to see their opinions as being largely genuine (and importantly, personally held). I got a distinct impression that they genuinely felt a desire to have the place develop into a community. They noted the involvement of Delfin and the *Springfield Community Centre* in the establishment of a 'Walking Bus' with a local school:

Nicole: ...so we're in the process of establishing a school walking bus. So people can—it's going to help address the obesity issue, it's getting the kids to school safely without having to worry about them because you've got a conductor and a driver; we just have to get the parents [involved]. That's the first hurdle is to get the support so we're looking at hoping to have that up and running by the first semester. So before Easter the principal wants to get the expressions of interest out before the school holidays. (Nicole and Debbie, 28th March 2007)

Nicole went on to note that there were no extrinsic incentives for Delfin to be involved in this, apart from having something positive for the students to be involved in.

Regardless of whether I was being sold a line by Nicole and Debbie, the sorts of ideas about community they raised were echoed by some of my other informants. Corey, a local police constable, noted that:

Corey: They [Springfield Community Centre and Delfin] organise a lot of community events. They make sure the community is all involved in there, and everything they do. It's very good.

Andrew: Does this help with Police work?

Corey: Sure. Makes it a lot more community oriented around here... It's going well.

I'd say it's different to other areas. Like this place here is attached to Goodna [a neighbouring and socio-economically depressed suburb], so it's all in the Goodna area. So in terms of the Goodna district, this would probably be the less troublesome place. (Corey, 12th November 2007)

Corey directly noted that community connection resulted in it being 'less troublesome' (which I took to mean that there was less crime). He noted that the inter-connectedness people had in Greater Springfield distinguished it from other areas and meant that its residents got along and looked out for each other.

This concern for personal safety emerged in discussions with several of my informants (informants who also happened to be parents of young families). Maree in particular identified this concern for community as a mechanism for ensuring safety in her neighbourhood:

Maree:	The other thing that I love is that my three boys are my eldest and then my three girls are my youngest. My boys are 11, 10 and 9, so they're old enough that here I trust that they can ride their bikes around and not be hit by a truck.
Andrew:	So a sense of safety is present?
Maree:	Yeah. I mean obviously I tell them they have to check in every half an hour, but they are allowed to ride with their friends, or ride up to their friend's house. And the fact that the school's here now, pretty much all their friends live within riding distance, which they love. It's good. (Maree, 21st November 2007)

Connectedness also featured as a significant aspect of Greater Springfield for Rebecca:

Rebecca:	I like that in terms of where I live I like people to know each other.
Andrew:	Is that a stereotypical or archetypal 'small town' idea of community?
Rebecca:	Yeah.
Andrew:	Where someone down the road knows you quite well; when you go to the shops you run into people from the neighbourhood....
Rebecca:	But then I suppose if you don't like that kind of thing you don't have to participate. (Rebecca, 25th September 2006)

While Delfin and the Springfield Land Corporation involvement in the creation of community was considered to be a largely positive thing by many of my informants, Brett, the attendant at a local music store, had reservations. He suggested that the idea of community as it was applied in Greater Springfield was a largely contrived one, and didn't represent an entirely democratic or participatory approach to community building:

Andrew:	If you had to put a definition on what community means in Springfield, what would it be?
Brett:	I don't think it's a community for mutual benefit. I think it's more of a community of similarities in that people get along here because everyone is so similar. It's kind of attracted such a specific 'moving up' demographic that you know people just get along...because they are the same. (Brett, 12th November 2007)

He went on to suggest that community formation in Greater Springfield is largely about the organisation of people on a class basis, and the transformation of space in Greater Springfield to meet these ends. He noted experiences he had in his store with customers identifying a distinction between instruments:

Brett:	As an example you see a lot of say people in their fifties walking to the shop and they walk in and they go straight over to the *grand* [grand piano]. They look at it and they sit at it.
Andrew:	They bypass the *Strats* [Fender Stratocaster electric guitars] and go straight over there?
Brett:	Oh yeah many of them go straight to that and they sit there and they look at it. So you know that's interesting. It's class.
Andrew:	Sure, so the grand is something to fill the living room up with?
Brett:	Well the fact that they actually have room to put a grand piano in is significant. *And most of them don't even play the piano so it's decadence.*
Andrew:	So it's suggestive of class, an economic capital, all those sorts of things?
Brett:	Yeah. (Brett, 12th November 2007, *emphasis added*)

He also noted that artifacts viewed as being culturally exotic were big sale items for this group of customers. In particular he had noted popularity for African drums:

| Brett: | We do sell *Djembe* drums...I swear every time we sell one it's to a mum and it's because she's going to go home and put in the corner as decoration. Yeah it's not because they play the drums. (Brett, 12th November 2007) |

I discuss the idea of affluence and cultural capital later in this chapter, but it was interesting to hear Brett talk about the distinction residents of Greater Springfield had for musical instruments. According to Brett, while it appeared that at least some of his customers didn't actually intend to play the instruments they purchased, they knew what the instruments expressed as decorative home-wares. This furthered his suggestion that community in Greater Springfield was a contrived, artificial community, where people were brought together not through a shared spatialisation, but under an economic process that filtered people according to the material wealth they demonstrated in the purchase of property and goods. These items then expressed a certain cultural capital; via artifacts such as grand pianos and djembe drums that *were never intended to be played* after purchase, a certain connection to a mode of living, or sense of distinction, was made.

Pre-fabricated Community

Following on from Brett's suggestions that there was an artificiality to community in Greater Springfield (where community became more of an amalgam of people from similar economic positions), several of my informants extended this idea to suggest that the pre-fabricated nature of community in Greater Springfield was attributable to its physicality and form. A concern shared by many of my informants suggested that *community*, unlike a building development, couldn't be so easily contrived and needed time to organically develop. Sharma noted this when suggesting:

Sharma: I think here is quite an unusual representation of community because it is a created community instead of a naturally created one.
I guess it seems to be where everything is in one location. There seems to be a sense of community and because it is in one location people do everything together. They educate their kids together, they socialise together and they go to church together. So it seems to be the fact that they're doing these things in the same place leads to that sense of community…like can't they see what they've created is synthetic; it's not natural? (Sharma, 4th April 2007)

Sharma's concern related to the way that specific groupings of people had been brought together. Much like Brett, she lamented the gentrification of the area and the economic variable that determined entry into the community. For her, this wasn't what community was about, and signified something 'synthetic', as she put it. Interestingly, she related the experiences of her parents in a development[4] in North Queensland, where she suggested a similar level of synthetic community had initially developed, but later decayed after input from the developer was withdrawn. Her concern for Greater Springfield was that, after the gloss had worn away, and the developers had moved on to the next project, the community may not be able to sustain its bonds. Rebecca also noted these concerns for the longevity of community and wondered what would happen after Delfin 'moved out'. She cited an example of an earlier development in south-east Queensland that she noted had stagnated and had since developed a reputation as being a 'bad' suburb. This connection between symbolic ideals such as community and physical spatiality was very significant in my discussions. Demonstrated in my informants' comments were clear connections between the physicality of space and the symbolic ideals of community. My informants were articulating a concern for how these two aspects of culture come together in Greater Springfield.

---

[4] As it happened, this too was a Delfin development focused variously towards young families and 'over 50s'.

In terms of the structure and spatiality of the built environment, several of my informants noted that convenience was an important aspect of life in Greater Springfield. John and Audrey, a couple I met while they waited for a taxi at the *Orion Shopping Centre* (the major retail hub in Greater Springfield), suggested the following:

Audrey:	I think it will be good. It's better for me, bank-wise, than going to Browns Plains [a neighbouring suburb]. It's easier parking and the banks are all in one line.
Andrew:	So there are a lot more services available here?
John:	Yeah. All the banks are here. St George [bank], we'd have to go to Logan or Jimboomba [surrounding suburbs] without them. (John and Audrey, 12th October 2007)

I couldn't help but think of the 'Convenience—what a refreshing change' street banner when I was talking to John and Audrey. While they appeared happy to talk to me, they didn't really have any opinions on what community was like in Greater Springfield other than that living here was convenient. This in some ways summed it up for me; the newness of this development and its array of shops and services had transformed this previously 'unwanted land' into something fitted out with the conveniences of a modern urban space. But at the same time that John and Audrey celebrated the fact that they had easy access to banks and shops, I realised that this place was only really built according to how contemporary lifestyles in a capitalist, Western country are lived (or more specifically, are *supposed* to be lived).

Community in Greater Springfield was manufactured and defined according to not only what its residents wanted but also *expected* as people long socialised into the ways of contemporary lifestyles. The development simultaneously responded to, but also reinforced contemporary modes of living, with part of this translating into how we come to understand community in contemporary (sub)urban spaces. John and Audrey's suggestion that convenience was important not only tapped the underlying themes of the marketing campaign deployed in Springfield Lakes, but also gave a poignant indication of what they considered as important in urban space more broadly. They were buying into the idea of this type of community as much as they represented the demographic of people who the marketers targeted in the first place; thus maintaining the self-fulfilling logic of the market. For me, John and Audrey's experiences weren't simply a case of the market responding to their needs for convenience. John and Audrey were actors in a situation that required them to live a mode of life that is responsible for the problems that this development sets out to solve (that is, the construction of an edge city like Greater Springfield that contains the sorts of services people like John and Audrey need). From within this logic, the perpetuation of set modes of living is guaranteed—no where in my conversations did I hear any suggestions for a rethink on how urban space is arranged and how lifestyles might be led in Greater Springfield. The logic of Greater Springfield, and urban living more generally, was maintained, even when my informants were being critical—they still framed their understandings of this development and contemporary urban living on *what it was*, not *what it could be*. But then again, Greater Springfield is, perhaps apart from its well-publicised points of distinctiveness including its open parklands and lakes, *newness* and shopping centres, fundamentally like any other urban/suburban space in Australia.

Rationalising the Artificiality of Community in Greater Springfield

The artificiality of the ideals of community presented in Greater Springfield was picked up specifically by Rebecca in several of our discussions. While she noted that she was very much attached to the place and felt a strong sense of connection and was initially sceptical of the way that a corporation was handling things like the development of themes of community, her opinion began to change as we progressed through our discussions with each other:

Andrew: Is it interesting or peculiar to you that Delfin is behind getting these clubs organized, and not say, the local council?

Rebecca: Yeah I think that is a peculiarity to Springfield because usually it would be the local council or a charity organization. But I suppose Delfin fill that void that would otherwise be here.

I suppose having some kind of community groups [those organised by Delfin and run from the *Springfield Lakes Community Centre*], especially for people who are home during the day such as stay at home mums or retirees enables them to feel a little bit less isolated because public transport is still a huge issue in this area—or lack thereof.

Andrew: What would the place look like if it didn't have these community groups and the input from Delfin do you think?

Rebecca: I think people as individuals would probably feel very isolated because I have heard that comment a couple of years ago from retirees that they felt really isolated, that there was nothing for them to do around here and getting a bus to anywhere took hours and hours. So I think that for the mental health of the community it's a really good idea. And also it gets people to know each other a little bit better and so I think they're trying to create and I think to a large extent it has been successful for whatever reason behind that, but successful in terms of encouraging community participation. (Rebecca, 23rd October 2006)

She noted two days later when I revisited this theme with her:

Rebecca:

I think it certainly means something. You know for all the cynicism you can have about a master-plan community it certainly—I would have—before I moved to Springfield, I would certainly have been very cynical about this type of community and not really happy or pleased to live in the suburbs but you know economics meant that I had to live in the suburbs. However, since living in this community I've been very happy because Delfin do supply a lot of community-based activities that the local council would not ever supply.

So if Delfin did not offer these activities there would be less and less and less. Now of course these activities—you can look behind what kind of activities are offered by Delfin but they still have opportunities for families, they have a lot of free concerts with really good kids programs....

So in terms of what they offer to the community it can be really good. And I think—and I think based on the fact that they do have activities for people that live in the community—I think that helps to foster a really good community spirit. (Rebecca, 25th October 2006)

It was typically in a manner similar to this that many of my informants rationalised the involvement of Delfin in the construction of community in Greater Springfield. While Jane and Brett were most vocal in their criticisms, Pete and Maree and John and Audrey as key examples acknowledged that what they saw in Greater Springfield was something positive. Even Rebecca, with whom I spent considerable time talking (virtually the duration of the project) about the way community was formed, acknowledged (after initial scepticism) that what Delfin had done was supply the infrastructure for community to operate. While my informants may have questioned the input of a corporation and its motives into the development of community, they conceded that what was in Greater Springfield worked to mitigate the isolation in the development. Reflecting on her experiences of Greater Springfield, Rebecca summed up this position in the following statement:

Rebecca:

But something occurred to me the other day, 'cause of course Springfield has got its problems and things like that and of course I'm very cynical anyway of master plan communities and I'm cynical of who determines what public spaces are considered important and so forth. But—and I have my reservations about a lot of things in Springfield I suppose, based on that.

But, why didn't—when someone the other day they criticised Springfield and they said some mean things about Springfield residents—like they don't care about the environment, the master plan community and so forth—and I found myself getting very defensive at the fact that someone would dare criticise *my* community. Even though I know that it's got a lot of problems and issues, just the thought that someone else would criticise it really upset me.

So I suppose the community that you live in despite its problems and I suppose it doesn't matter which community you're in, in Australia, whether it's in a remote community or the city or the fringe or the metropolitan, if you feel ownership over your community you have a certain sense of pride whether or not that pride is misplaced or not I suppose.

So the kinds of artificially created senses of community that are probably mocked by some people within this community, but other people I think really believe in it. (Rebecca, 7th November 2007)

While she may not have agreed with everything that Delfin had done and the imposition by a corporation into ideas of community, it was still *her* community, and from that a very specific and acknowledged connectedness had formed. It was positions similar to this that I found most of the people I talked to in Greater Springfield held.

A Sense of Community

It was evident from what my informants were telling me that a distinct sense of community, as McMillan and Chavis (1986) would define it, was present in Greater Springfield. But just as Rebecca had noted that she felt sceptical about the corporate involvement in the development of community, when discussing how they actually *enacted* community my informants generally didn't refer to the sorts of ideals presented by the billboards and brochures distributed by the developers. While Maree noted that having services available was useful, and Rebecca cited the community groups as a positive demonstration of collectivity, the general response to my questions about how people actually went about *living* community generally didn't feature Delfin and Springfield Land Corporation ideals. Mike identifies this cogently:

Mike: But we've got two young children just started at the new school here and that's helped I think; the new school. We'll be up the street and you know the little daughter will see all her friends and all that sort of stuff. It's a good street and we're all friends and we get out and have a beer or whatever.
Andrew: That's an important thing do you think?
Mike: Absolutely, yeah. (Mike, 21st November 2007)

It became clear that two parallel ideals of community were expressed in Greater Springfield; one idealised in the development's signage and another lived in an everyday, 'ordinary' way by residents who 'get out and have a beer'.

Occasionally these parallel ideals of community converged and the line between them blurred. Rebecca noted one particularly significant demonstration of this when she described the construction of a bridge over a small gully in *Augustine Heights* upon which residents could purchase a plaque commemorating their 'founding' of the area:

Rebecca:	So they've got this little gully bridge and it's stone—it's near the *Catherine Morgan Park*—if you go there you see plaques with these people's names on it.
Andrew:	So the fact the bridge is made out of stone and you've got the plaques on it, what does that suggest? What does that signify?
Rebecca:	That its a 'country idyllic lifestyle', yeah, and that its peaceful that you've come away from the stressful life of your city job whatever and people actually bought those plaques and put their names on them.
Andrew:	I'm getting, and tell me if I'm wrong here, but I'm getting the imagery of sort of like a Lakes District, English village almost....
Rebecca:	Yeah, I suppose so.
Andrew:	Is it also that core people, your 'founding' core families identified and you know who they are and those core families are central to the community as pillars of the community; the physical manifestations of this is that they're named on the plaque?
Rebecca:	Yeah...but then they paid for it.
Andrew:	In the Augustine Heights case, because there is no real tradition there—because it's a brand new place—is this a construction of tradition perhaps?
Rebecca:	It certainly is. (Rebecca, 7th November 2007)

In this instance community as a desire of the developers met head on with those local people who were happy to pay to have their version of tradition and community listed on the bridge. This was the sort of complexity that ideas of community threw up in Greater Springfield. As I noted above, it wasn't a simple dualism between residents' ideas of community versus the developers'. Residents were simultaneously sceptical and supportive of how community had been pre-formed in Greater Springfield. They also deployed their own interpretations of it in the form of neighbourhood gatherings as much as they engaged with community groups and the purchase of a plaque for a bridge. Community in Greater Springfield became a pastiche—an amalgam of what suited residents at given points in time. However, while this might appear to suggest an agency on behalf of residents and their ability to 'pick and mix' their ideals of community, it remained that what community was considered to be was still informed by the types of residents

Greater Springfield attracted and how conceptualisations of what community *should* be in the contemporary world had socialised these people. The bridge upon which residents' names were attached was still an authorised part of the development, after all.

Community People: Being Old/Being Young

After I began to get a sense of *what* community was in Greater Springfield, I turned my questions to *who* my informants thought it was for. It quickly emerged that my informants felt there were two groups of people Greater Springfield was targeted towards; young families and retirees. Nicole noted this when talking about recent experiences:

Nicole:	I mean [Graham and Christina—a retired couple] are a perfect example. They are a couple in the 'leisure group' [an 'over-50s' group] and a young family moved in beside them—they were the surrogate grandma, grandad for this family.
Andrew:	Were both families away from their extended family?
Debbie:	Yes.
Nicole:	And it works well and it just makes them feel comfortable at home. And it's good for the senior peoples to know that somebody younger, if anything happens, can call on them; I can call on them to watch the kids for half an hour for example. (Nicole and Debbie, 28th March 2007)

This vision of the Greater Springfieldian typified the demographic of residents expressed by most of my informants; typically, older retired couples and young families. But this conceptualisation of who the Greater Springfieldian is excluded anyone who wasn't old and wasn't in a young family. Teenagers in particular became a focus of this exclusion, and Rebecca noted this on a couple of occasions. On one of our first meetings she noted the popularity of the sole piece of public space in Greater Springfield intended for teenagers; the skateboard park:

Rebecca:	See I think the one good thing about Springfield [for teenagers] is the skateboard park. That's it to me. Yeah there is graffiti in the skateboard park because that's what—to me that's what a skateboard park is though. It's an opportunity for young people to have ownership over an area and to tag it in ways they see fit.
Andrew:	To identify themselves and identify and mark the space.
Rebecca:	They're not tagging trees or anything. They're just tagging the cement that they're skateboarding on but to me that's the one greatest part of Springfield because that's—the current skate park is on a main road and it's well lit. It's next to Coles [supermarket] and next to take away shops and it's next to a big football oval.

I think that's—and there's always young kids around there and it's also often parents of the younger kids around there too and it just seems to me to be somewhere that young people really can go to chill out but in a safe area because they can be observed at all times so there's less opportunities for people with undesirable intentions to be there like drug pushers and things like that. Which isn't to say that doesn't happen but.... (Rebecca, 23rd October 2006)

She then went on to note that, as she saw it, very little was done for young people in Greater Springfield:

Rebecca: I also think more needs to be done to encourage young people of the high school and just post high school age to have activities and things to do on weeknights and weekends because I think Springfield as a satellite suburb or satellite city that people are isolated.
If you don't have transport there's not very much that you can do in Springfield for that age group and I think it's inappropriate to say that young people can just stay at home studying or go to the library....

Andrew: So the suggestion is for young people to somehow occupy themselves with limited resources?

Rebecca: Or play sport and so forth because I think there's a lot more issues associated with—I think young people need a place to be able to hang out more. I wouldn't like to be a teenager in Springfield.

Andrew: Because of the isolation factor again?

Rebecca: Yeah I think being a teenager in Springfield would probably suck. (Rebecca, 23rd October 2006)

She followed this up a couple of days later by noting:

Rebecca: So that young family idea that you mentioned as *the* Springfield family sort of taps into that marketing dynamic. But when, as you've just done, you survey a street it shows something a little bit different perhaps. And look there are a lot of retired couples or a lot of semi-retired people and there are a lot of...community organisations within Delfin for those people. But say young people, people like myself may not have as many opportunities for entertainment. Retirees...there's things on for them. (Rebeca, 25th September 2006)

It followed that just as there was a certain idea about what community was in Greater Springfield, that similarly specific ideas about *who* was in the community were also held. My informants, particularly Rebecca, were quite specific about Greater Springfield being for young families and retirees and noted that other groups divided on lines of age weren't so well catered to. For me, the last word rests with Debbie, the representative from Delfin, when she noted that:

Debbie: Yeah I think it's a community hub and you know you're welcome
                           when residents say we just feel like we're on holidays here every
                           day; we love it; we love the lake; we love coming to the coffee
                           shop....
                           (Nicole and Debbie, 28th March 2007)

The question for me, and as it appeared for Rebecca also, was what happened if you didn't love the lake, or going to the coffee shop; what if your interests due to your age demographic meant that other things were in your interests? It seemed that unless the skate park was your 'thing', there wasn't much else available for these 'alternative' Greater Springfieldians. Again, Maha Sinnathamby's ideas (as noted earlier) resonate; that young people should engage in study and sport (and not much else). Here were clear expressions as to what one subset of the demographic was 'supposed' to be within the confines of Greater Springfield's physical space.

Wealth, Affluence and Cultural Capital

Furthering the identification of the *typical* Greater Springfieldian, my informants also noted that this was very much an affluent middle-class location. Pete, the commercial painter I met while he took his morning tea break, noted:

Pete: Yeah, well you've got to have the money. To afford to live here
                           you've got to have a fair bit of money behind you. Move up, find
                           your uplifting place—same thing, isn't it? Get yourself into more
                           debt I suppose. (Pete, 21st November 2007)

The fact that he parodied the slogan from the billboard that towered over us on the roadside near where we were seated was significant. He had read the sign as being specifically suggestive of the sort of attitude that worked through Greater Springfield. In particular, he saw it as being explicitly connected to wealth and the ability to finance the sort of lifestyle Greater Springfield offered. Natalie, a resident I met whilst she was shopping at Orion Shopping Centre, also noted the level of affluence and class locatedness Greater Springfield suggested:

Natalie: Definitely. I mean people can pay the same amount for a house in
                           Springfield that you could in inner city Brisbane—the blocks of
                           land are tiny—so they are obviously looking—whatever

Springfield is offering, that is what they're looking for because it is not cheap. It is not cheap to buy here. (Natalie, 4th April 2007)

She went on to suggest that the newness and 'community-oriented planning' (which I took to mean the way that centralised public space was incorporated into the master plan) attracted people to the area, and alluded to the sense of community that seemed to exist within the area. In any case, my informants generally agreed that this was an expensive place to live and represented a location of affluent middle-class aspiration.

But my informants also identified the stratification that existed within Greater Springfield as well; this was no homogenous place. Toula suggested that the different areas and sub-developments within Greater Springfield were targeted toward different groups of people according to the style and price of housing available:

Andrew: Do you find socio-economic subsets in the community?

Toula: Definitely and you've got a variety of housing here so you've got your Springfield Lakes, you've got your Brookwater which is the really expensive golf course. But you've also got quite a high proportion, I think, from what I can gather, of rental properties...and of course we're really close to Camira which has very cheap house prices and all that sort of stuff.

Andrew: Is there a divide there? Is there a cultural divide between the older and the new parts of the development?

Toula: Oh definitely and the kids that come from there. They are probably the rental properties and all that sort of thing. I mean I find it bizarre that Brookwater is built right next to Goodna which is a really low socio economic and then you've got million dollar homes in Brookwater. I find that strange.

Andrew: It doesn't make sense at all does it?

Toula: But maybe that is just me because I don't understand the way that these things develop. I don't know but I just find there are huge disparities which are created by Delfin so you're going to have the same social problems aren't you? It is not going to clear things up automatically. (Toula, 4th April 2007)

Several of the informants identified a distinction between Brookwater and the rest of Greater Springfield. It appeared that Brookwater was clearly identified as being exclusive by being a 'prestige' location, as Barry and Jeff, representatives of a local construction company, noted:

Barry: So yeah the big thing I mean Brookwater started to market in the early stages. I mean that started six years ago I think. They started trying to market to the affluent sort of suburbs as in the western suburbs who had money. People thought yeah we'll pull them out of Brisbane. It's not too far it's probably 15 to 20 minutes. It just didn't work. They didn't get anywhere with it so they started marketing towards Ipswich and they pulled a lot of—I mean Ipswich didn't really have a suburb that was your upmarket, top of the hill.

Andrew: So Brookwater sort of filled that role?

Barry: I think so yeah. I always think that they've fulfilled the sort of prestige market at Ipswich which I don't know any other places that do it. I mean secondary to that would be obviously here and now, well I mean it's all brand new suburbs but out of these new suburbs of Springfield and us, Brookwater would be your sort of upmarket prestige area. (Barry and Jeff, 12th November 2007)

Mike, a young dad I met while he was spending time with his children in a Springfield Lakes park, similarly identified the 'upmarket' nature of Brookwater, but also gave his thoughts on *who* the Brookwater resident was:

Andrew: Brookwater—what does that say to you?

Mike: It says it's too expensive for me. It's a bit too ritzy for me. That's what it says.

Andrew: Is there an age differential tied into the development do you think?

Mike: I think so. I think this is more you know, older professional type people.

Andrew: People looking to settle down or retire?

Mike: I'd say, you know, a doctor or a lawyer lives there. Yeah so again, not typical of what you see and the folks I know in my street? (Mike, 21st November 2007)

Rebecca also suggested that Brookwater is fundamentally different to the rest of Greater Springfield. She identified that the affluence, class location and expression of exclusivity that derived from it, made it something different from the rest of Greater Springfield:

Rebecca: As a Springfield resident I don't see Brookwater as part of Springfield because of its exclusivity and its detachment from the main part of Springfield you actually have to more or less travel out of Springfield to get to Brookwater. I don't consider it to be part of Springfield although I know that some Brookwater residents may consider themselves to be part of Springfield.

Andrew: Or vice-versa perhaps?

Rebecca: Yeah but it—Brookwater seems like another—a different place.

Andrew: Is there a connection do you think between each of these different locations? We've also got—the development further up the road heading towards....

Rebecca: Brentwood.

Andrew: Yes, so do these places need to work together do you think to set

Rebecca:

up an overall identity or can they have their own individual identities that may even be competing?

I think the idea—I mean Brentwood isn't in Springfield, it's in Bellbird Park so I think though that Brookwater just from its advertising and so forth wants to be separate from Springfield because it sets itself up very much to be like that way and I suppose Augustine Heights may as well separate itself from Springfield intentionally to have a different identity and to try and promote exclusivity or...a class-economic difference or something. (Rebecca, 23rd October 2006)

What was emerging from these discussions was a clear identification by residents of Greater Springfield of a hierarchy of suburban locations within the larger development. Rebecca confirmed this a couple of days later when I revisited this theme of difference between the suburbs:

Rebecca:

Yeah there's certainly different hierarchies associated I think in people's minds about depending on the part of Springfield they live in. So as you know like I've told you before when [my friend] asked me where I lived and I said Springfield and they said Springfield Lakes or Springfield?

Andrew:

Right, so there's a distinction between *Old* Springfield and Springfield Lakes?

Rebecca:

And when I said Springfield they told me that I was 'pov' [poor]! They said how I was pov for where I lived and so I suppose...

Andrew:

So it's definitely a mindset that people have?

Rebecca:

I think it could be a mindset that some people have definitely. So you've got Springfield, then Springfield Lakes and I suppose Augustine Heights and then Brookwater. That's probably how it goes on the hierarchy. (Rebecca, 25th October 2006)

There was certainly an implicit understanding amongst those people I spoke with that each of the different suburbs within Greater Springfield had its own place in the 'hierarchy' (as Rebecca noted). It went without saying that ownership in a certain location carried cultural significance and said something about who you were—primarily how much money you had.

But just as with the ideas that were captured in the billboards and brochures that accompanied the different developments, ideals of style and distinction were seen by my informants to be carried through the property ownership decisions people had made. As an example, while Mike may have been condescending in his accounts of a Brookwater lifestyle and his summation that it was 'doctors and lawyers' who lived there, he still attributed a certain identity to the place and its residents, and by comparison identified his neighbourhood in Springfield Lakes as being something different. Regardless of how accurate this attribution was, in his mind (and in the minds of most informants as it turned out) specific types of people lived in each of the suburban spaces of Greater Springfield. This clear understanding by my informants of who lived where followed much the same logic as the artifacts I explored in the previous chapter; the brochures and other artifacts carried implicit suggestions of lifestyle choice that were echoed by residents who knew the *codes* of Greater Springfield ownership choice. It seemed that here was a case where the ideals of each suburb— Brookwater and Springfield Lakes in particular—were captured by the signs of Greater Springfield and relayed by the residents in almost identical fashion.

Distinction and Cultural Capital

According to my informants, it emerged that being in Greater Springfield was different from being in those economically depressed areas that surrounded it. But just as importantly, certain areas within Greater Springfield also suggested certain things about the residents that occupied these spaces. Rebecca identified these assumptions when she noted:

Rebecca:

But I don't know anyone that refers to themselves as living in Ipswich because there's—because people that live in Springfield, if you want to be stereotypical, are aspirational—and there is a negative social connotation of saying that you live in Ipswich. In fact, I used to teach in a local high school and one of the students was bagging out people that live in Ipswich so I decided to remind the class that they live in Ipswich.

I had some very upset students; very upset students and one student yelled at me and told me that they don't live in Ipswich, *what would I know?* They were quite shocked about the fact that they actually lived within the boundaries of Ipswich and they had no idea, even though their parents get...the city council rates, the signs on the streets have Ipswich City Council etc...they think Springfield is its own city. (Rebecca, 7th November 2007)

Rebecca suggested that this process of self-identification is largely attributable to the marketing of the place and the way that the development of Greater Springfield has been celebrated almost in isolation to those areas surrounding it. She identified an insularity that pervades Greater Springfield, and titled this phenomenon '*the Delfin effect*', which I'll explore later in this chapter.

My informants were broadly referring to a sense of distinction that residence in Greater Springfield afforded. This connection to ideals of style and taste suggests that residents identified themselves via a cultural capital that presented in terms of a sense of distinction. What this meant was that to be in Greater Springfield carried certain emphases on ideals of affluence, wealth and sophistication. Brett's experiences in the music store when non-musicians came in to size up the grand piano and djembe drums for the 'spare room' stood as a clear expression of this. While these people weren't musicians, they attributed a cultural significance to these things and understood them to carry a sense of style or sophistication that an electric guitar, or something distinctively 'lesser', couldn't. However arbitrarily these conventions of style were attributed to artifacts like grand pianos, my informants noted that Greater Springfield contained within it a clear sense of what was significant within its cultural capital.

In trying to explain the origins of the cultural capital presented in Greater Springfield, Louise, a young woman I met in a Springfield Lakes park, noted that:

Louise:	There are certainly similar tensions that I guess you would see in any area such as tensions of class and how those different groups interact within the community. So what seems to dominate their behaviour is more to do with the class and socio cultural background than the actual location. The fact that they're in Springfield doesn't seem to change.... (Louise, 4th April 2007)

Rebecca and several of my other informants mentioned similar things to Louise, and identified the contrived nature of the community and the way that specific demographic segments of people had been targeted for Greater Springfield resulted in a concentration of specific values. Rather than being something that was already there, my informants suggested that the sense of distinction and style permeating Greater Springfield *came with* its residents. The shock with which Rebecca's students recoiled when it was suggested that they resided within the boundaries of the city of Ipswich stands as a key example. Ipswich, in terms of style and sophistication, was something other than what Greater Springfield represented in the minds of its residents, regardless of how the geographic delineations of space had organised them. To me, this was a clear expression of the self-consciousness of the area; Greater Springfield expressed a thoroughly middle-class aesthetic that Ipswich as a traditionally working-class 'mining town' couldn't accommodate. For Greater Springfieldians, Ipswich was the poor cousin they tried to distance themselves from.

The Public Pedagogies of Greater Springfield

The way that the residents of Greater Springfield came to understand their community's identity drew on a number of sources. While Louise suggested that a middle-class aesthetic that presented ideals of style, distinction and affluence as key indicators came into Greater Springfield with its residents, it remained that there was a concerted effort on behalf of the developers and their marketing agencies to attract this demographic segment in the first place. I explored some of those paleosymbolic ideals deployed to attract a certain market segment in the previous chapter.

What I was interested in knowing was how the residents viewed this process. When I met with Nicole and Debbie, two people actively involved in developing the identity of Greater Springfield through their work with Delfin, they noted that what they were trying to do was connect 'likeminded people'. Particularly in their role as community liaisons, Nicole and Debbie were actively involved in supporting and providing assistance for the various community groups that operated in Greater Springfield. As they noted, their role was to assist in getting these groups off the ground:

Nicole: So that's the first thing and then from there it is a matter of sort of through our job is trying to establish more community groups and trying to connect likeminded people for the social side of things or for the educational side of things. So it's all within the—in the hub. (Nicole and Debbie, 27th March 2007)

While it made perfect sense to get similar people involved in activities and community events, it also suggested to me that this sort of involvement by the developers in crafting social networks could potentially result in the creation of insularity that Rebecca had noted, or the outright isolation that Jane experienced. It seemed to me that it all hinged on what sort of groups and activities the developers were happy to support, as this would give an indication of what types of people they considered to be Greater Springfieldians. While Nicole and Debbie both suggested that, on a couple of occasions during our meetings, they would be happy to support any group that residents suggested would be useful, I asked them whether an *Islamic Literature Reading Group*, for instance, would be possible to form. The response was that they suspected there wouldn't be enough interest to sustain such a group, which left me to conclude that between the middle-class aesthetic that residents brought with them into the area and the initial marketing towards a specific demographic of buyers by the developers, a very clear sense of what was 'normal' was established. If you didn't fit this set of identity characteristics, as Jane had found, the experience of Greater Springfield could become a very isolated one.

The role of signs is centrally important here. Within the sorts of images, text and implicit themes they presented were suggestions of the types of lifestyle and people Greater Springfield celebrated. I asked my informants what they thought about this process, and whether or not they felt the billboards, brochures and other artifacts exerted a pressure on the identity of Greater Springfield and its people. Brett felt that the way Greater Springfield was advertised exerted a direct influence over what it was:

Brett: I think when people come to Springfield they're buying into the idea of the community.
Andrew: You mentioned advertising; do you think it's solely advertising that's doing this? That perhaps it's advertising that's constructed an image that people have seen and said; 'yes that's me'?
Brett: I think the advertising attracts the type of people who want to be in a part of a community so it perpetuates a community because you're attracting people who want to participate in the community. (Brett, 12th November 2007)

Building on this theme, Rebecca drew attention to the use of 'actual' residents in the signage of Greater Springfield (a theme I referred to in the previous chapter). She suggested that the way signage came to present ways of life was a significant extension of the logic deployed in Greater Springfield by its developers:

Andrew: [Nicole and Debbie] mentioned that the people represented in the ads are actual residents of the lakes?
Rebecca: Yes, that's true. Yeah definitely because you see them around—I mean you see them walking around or might know them because you've taught their kids or whatever. But yeah they are definitely residents of the lakes but they're carefully selected.
Andrew: OK, so how are they selected?
Rebecca: They're selected because they know someone at Delfin by and large. Like I've never seen an ad in the paper that says we're trying out for a—auditioning for a commercial; they know the people. (Rebecca, 29th March 2007)

Rebecca was sceptical of the hand-selected nature of this advertising. These 'real people' as Nicole and Debbie labelled them, may well have been residents (and for that matter 'real' people and not paid actors), but for Rebecca the hand-selected nature of their inclusion said something about the desire the developers had to show a certain type of individual as resident in Greater Springfield. For Rebecca, the very white, middle-class, heterosexual and nuclear family arrangement displayed in the billboards and brochures didn't capture a genuine image of what *her* Greater Springfield was. As she noted:

Rebecca: I mean on the ads it's really promoted—I have never seen anyone except for a white person who looks like they ascribe to middle-class values. I mean just looking at my own street that I live in, I

	live in a small cul-de-sac, there are probably about 10 houses in my whole street.
	So we've got a retired couple, we've got a mixed family—by mixed I mean step family like mum and dad have remarried but have combined their children. There's an old couple and a young couple as well. There's another young family. There's a Samoan family that live on the end of our street. Then there's another family with two kids and then there's another couple with a dog. A family from New Zealand.
Andrew:	Well that's an interesting mix isn't it? It doesn't necessarily add up with what the advertising image says.
Rebecca:	No it doesn't. (Rebecca, 25th September 2006)

While a concerted effort appears to have been made by the developers to present 'real people', for Rebecca those real people only represented a small subset of the people who lived in Greater Springfield. As I saw it during my time in Greater Springfield, this was a clear expression of the privileging of certain identity characteristics. More so, what the signs were doing included not only selling an image but also more explicitly suggested that the image being sold was in fact 'real'. And to a certain extent it was; but after looking closely, it was apparent that it was real for only a small sub-set of those people who called Greater Springfield home. This was a privileging of a specific lifestyle and identity; one that people like Jane and Brett couldn't relate to, and in the case of Jane specifically, felt isolated because of.

The 'Delfin Effect'

Just as isolation from the community was felt by Jane, my informants also noted that there existed an insularity amongst those residents who were included. Rebecca and Louise in particular identified a phenomenon they titled '*the Delfin effect*'. Labelled the Delfin effect because of the perceived insulation Delfin developments were attributed with, Rebecca and Louise suggested that it was those very factors that Delfin promoted that led to the rise of the effect. Louise suggested that the way Greater Springfield had been presented as a place 'you never need to leave' resulted in people's attitudes to the world being somewhat 'naïve and ill-formed'. Rebecca explained the effect in the following way:

Rebecca:	*The Delfin effect* is a catch phrase that has been applied to some of the students who live in a Delfin community and also attend Delfin community school because one of the highlights of living in Delfin community as portrayed in advertisements is that you never have to leave the community; everything is within this community.
Andrew:	That's seen as being a very positive thing in the advertisements as

	well.
Rebecca:	Yeah it is; like everything is within—all the shopping that you need, all the cultural activities you need, all the schools you know from birth to university is within a community. It's really set up as a satellite city within a larger metropolitan area. So from this I have noticed in some students that they—in the local high schools that they don't have an awareness of the world around them and seem to only exist within the world they have immediate contact with.
	So as a result they have a…social literacy deficit in that they don't understand the surrounding city or the surrounding state or the surrounding nation that they live in and this has detriments on their education but this—and whilst you might find this in a lot of areas that students may not know so much about the world around them in the broader context.
	The difference that some teachers have noticed with students in the local area is that they seem to be proud of this fact and that it's not a cause for embarrassment or a cause for wanting to learn more. It is actually seen as almost a badge of honour that they know so little about the world around them. (Rebecca, 25th September 2006)

She continued in a later interview by suggesting:

Rebecca:	I think when big business says you never have to leave the community that we have created I think it encourages ignorance and encourages people to think oh at a subconscious level perhaps *I don't need to know anything else because I know all I need to know to live and operate in my small world.*
Andrew:	So there might be a danger then in having a community that does offer everything you need?
Rebecca:	Yeah I—and I say often that whenever I hear the Delfin ad of *oh you never have to leave Springfield Lakes* I think well that's more reason to leave Springfield Lakes so that you do have an understanding of the world around you and have an understanding of difference and what goes on outside your small suburb. (Rebecca, 25th September 2007)

Rebecca put the operation of *the Delfin effect* down to the geographic isolation of Greater Springfield and the concerted effort the developers had made to present it as a place that contained everything. In two separate discussions, she noted the following:

Rebecca:	At the moment if a young person wants to go into Brisbane city they would have to walk to the bus stop which might take five minutes, then catch the bus say to the Coles at Springfield down to Goodna which would take 20 minutes, 20 minutes to half an hour.

If they live in Springfield Lakes certainly it'd take the full 30 minutes there. Then they would have to catch the train to Goodna to the city and that would take 35 minutes.

So just to get that far is over an hour and that—the bus service operates a few times per day so maybe once an hour or once every hour and a half. So I think young people are really isolated. I would like to see more activities offered to young people to encourage their participation. Goodna does have some so that's good but it's also difficult to get to Goodna at times for some people. (Rebecca, 25th September 2007)

Rebecca:

I look at those ads that talk about community—and there are residents that say things like—*oh I don't ever need to leave Springfield*. I look at those with disdain—they're terrible ads because you do have to leave Springfield, but even if you don't *need* to leave a city or a town or whatever else, because they've got all the services there—well that doesn't mean that you *shouldn't* leave and probably gives more reason to actually get out and broaden your horizons a little bit more. (Rebecca, 7th November 2007)

For Rebecca and Louise, *the Delfin effect* worked hand in hand with the signs that promoted Greater Springfield as a self-sufficient and self-sustaining location. This became apparent to me when I looked around the place, looked at its billboards and signage and realised that it was insulated—and actively so.

Far from being something shameful and to be embarrassed about, insularity in Greater Springfield, as Rebecca noted, was something to be proud of. It signified a type of loyalty to community and suggested that all that needed to be known was within Greater Springfield. I couldn't help but think that it was all a bit too *Stepford Wives-ish* for my liking—particularly as I looked at its billboards and spoke to residents who told me that it was fantastic and that they were indeed 'afraid of travelling outside of Greater Springfield' (Maree, 21st November 2007) due to traffic and the fast pace of Brisbane.

The significant theme that emerged from the discussions I had with Rebecca and Louise about the Delfin effect was the influence they felt the billboards, brochures and advertising of Greater Springfield had. In this sense, these were very much public pedagogical artifacts that exerted a very specific view; a celebration of insularity and an associated set of ideals for the identity of the community and the types of people who reside within it. I kept coming back to the point that Louise made when she suggested that this was a 'strange' place. Indeed it was; to me and people like Jane and to a lesser extent Rebecca, Brett and Louise.

But it seemed that the insularity and specific identity characteristics that were celebrated in Greater Springfield did make sense to a lot of people; they *chose* to live there after all. But again, it all came back to the logic of the signage and the public pedagogical expressions of sets of ideals. The influence of these ideals was in the attraction they provided to those people who went on to fulfill them.

Chapter 5

Tying It All Together: Public Pedagogy, Urban Space and the Logic of the Now

> An enquiry into the inner meaning of specifically modern life and its products, into the soul of the cultural body, so to speak, must seek to solve the equation which structures like the metropolis set up between the individual and the supra-individual contents of life.
>
> —Georg Simmel, *The Metropolis and Mental Life*

So where does all this leave Greater Springfield? I presented in previous chapters an analysis of how various ideals came to be represented in Greater Springfield via such *everyday* communication artifacts as billboards and brochures, and juxtaposed these ideals against various residents' experiences of the place. I suggested that selected expressions of things such as *community* and *belonging* were privileged due to an authorized presence on the landscape and furthered this premise by arguing that the expressions of specific ideals carried by signage exerted a publicly pedagogical role. That is, these selected ideas about community, family, distinction, lifestyle, belonging, etc., not only functioned as collectively recognized points of meaning but were central in framing the very logic of the cultural milieu. Deployed on host billboards, and in brochures, newspaper advertisements and other media, the ideals being presented operated paleosymbolically in their suggestions of what life was like in Greater Springfield and what sort of person went about living it. I argued that these signs moved beyond being simple marketing tools to become iconic and formative cultural artifacts.

These artifacts became expressions of the logic of Greater Springfield— that location of symbolic meaning construction signified by the way elements of the physical environment became configured to mean. The formulation of the logic of Greater Springfield was, like so many locations of late-capitalism, mediated heavily by the mass culture-economic complex of the contemporary, globalized world, with the ubiquity and everyday-ness of things like billboards and brochures going some way to mask the corporate intentions that lurked behind much of what happened. Whilst 'ordinary' they may be, these signs-as-artifacts function as active 'carriers of ideology' (Harper 2006: 215), and as such must be critiqued and opened for scrutiny. To simply see signs as part of the landscape, and to fail to question the influence they are designed to exert, is to miss the point.

A blurring of the lines between outright marketing tool and social networking device occurred with many of the artifacts I looked at. This was particularly noticeable with the *'Community Update'* brochures, in which community information and advertising of Springfield Land Corporation and Delfin events and products were intertwined as roughly one and the same thing. Even the billboards, those image-rich, and usually text-poor mass communication devices, deployed throughout Greater Springfield contained more than just advertising. Paleosymbolic and highly philosophical statements on how to live were suggested in their calls to *'move up'* and challenges to *'compromise'*, albeit with the ever-present implication that to do these things meant succumbing to their intentions by purchasing property in this place.

Yet, deciphering these signs wasn't simply a case of working out what was advertising and what was philosophical statement. They were both at once, and contained views about the place at the same time as they sold it to residents and intending residents. Advertising *became* information (and information advertising) in the nexus of corporatized communitarianism presented in Greater Springfield. This was the state of the logic in Greater Springfield, and while these signs presented as important community information disseminators, they were also *just* marketing tools. While they contained various lifestyle suggestions implied in ideals of choice and belonging, leisure and relaxation, affluence and comfortable living, their reason for being was to present particular images of the place that sold property. This was, after all, the Springfield Land Corporation's and Delfin's development, and it was they who authorised the suggestions of what it was to *be* via the marketing campaigns they deployed. At best, these expressions of an *infotainment-like* blurring of actual public interest information and blatant advertising carried simple public information messages (such as examples of water safety messages, or gardening tips included in several *Springfield Lakes Community Updates*). But underlying these, as components of a discursive apparatus that had a very clear marketing imperative, were intentions to present and *sell* Greater Springfield in very defined ways.

As part of the landscape of Greater Springfield I saw these signs actively mediating how the development would function. Within the expressions of lifestyle, affluence and leisure expressed via the imagery and text embedded within each sign, the logic of Greater Springfield was cast and presented ready for consumption. These artifacts naturally worked hand in hand with the underlying intentions for the development (they provided the mechanism through which the developers' intentions functioned) by affirming the types of lifestyles and people Greater Springfield would support. From the consistently framed visions presented by the artifacts, ideas about the physical environment, the nature of community and its people were established in the public imagination of Greater Springfield.

The Pedagogy of the Public in Greater Springfield

I argued that these expressions of contemporary mass culture became pedagogical via their intent to present a specific set of identity characteristics and suggestions of what life *could* be like in Greater Springfield. It was via these expressions of life that characteristic features of who *the* Greater Springfieldian was, and how that archetype went about living, were presented to the world. I found there to be a largely consistent view of what the Greater Springfield lifestyle consisted of. My analysis of the lifestyle behaviours, attitudinal dispositions and identity locations expressed in the artifacts identified a clear sense of who the *right sort of person* for the place was, with the options available for this archetypal Greater Springfieldian being mostly limited to a specific set of racial/ethnic, class and gender/sexuality attributes.

The ideals underpinning the archetypal Greater Springfieldian weren't suggested forcibly—there weren't any check-boxes to tick that affirmed whether you were in or out—and I'm not trying to suggest that the billboards and brochures of Greater Springfield exerted an automatic attitude-altering influence over the people who viewed them. Nothing in culture is that easily transferable and to suggest that it is would be to deny any ability for individuals to accept, alter or resist the meanings being suggested according to their own interpretative agency. But via processes of what I call *passive selection* (namely, the largely accepted and rarely challenged economically derived selection process that authorizes entry into or exclusion from the markets of consumer capitalism—including that of home ownership) that mediate the relative ability intending residents had to not only purchase property but to also define where they purchased it, clear indicators of the type of person welcome in Greater Springfield were applied. You had to be the sort of person with the right amount of income to purchase into the Greater Springfield vision; it wasn't a place for just anyone to come in willy-nilly. Combined with these economic tropes, extended identity locations related to race/ethnicity, gender and class were largely consistent with an *affluent middle-class-ness* (as I noted in previous chapters). It was a very white, affluent and heterosexual world suggested by the artifacts, with limited possibilities for anything outside of this presented. But this wasn't the only mechanism deployed to identify the right type of person for Greater Springfield.

While economic determinants, extended by identity locations archetypally associated with an affluent middle-class, figured heavily in identifying the types of individual Greater Springfield became an investment option for, so too did the sense of style and distinction presented by the place. While the cultural capital of Greater Springfield varied in each sub-section within it (it became clear from looking around and talking to my informants that *Brookwater* was different from the *Escarpment*, for instance), broadly speaking this was a place that contained an aesthetic that complemented its economic determinants. The way leisure came to be identified through coffee-shop chic, the expression of cultural pursuits such as having a grand piano in the sitting room of a multi story home and concern for '*success*' as an outcome of financial wealth defined the logic of this aesthetic. As I noted in *Chapter 3*, the billboards and brochures displayed throughout Greater Springfield captured this intent, and taken together, fulfilled a pedagogical role to express specific ideals as being attributable to the place. My discussions with informants like Brett, Jane and Rebecca told me that 'real' expressions of this middle-class aesthetic were lived by at least some of Greater Springfield's residents and corresponded to a sense of distinction that pervaded the sorts of lifestyle that could be led in the place.

The down side of this of course is that if you didn't fit this aesthetic you simply couldn't belong. Aside from the processes of urban development that transformed this place that 'nobody wanted' into an expression of a 600m2 middle-class dream, isolation and exclusion did occur even if you did have the requisite money to buy in. Jane stood as a key example of this—she didn't see herself expressed in the billboards and brochures and found the reality of Greater Springfield to be oppressive. Brett also expressed his concern for the way a sense of arrogance circulated through the place and referred to the form of cultural capital presented in Greater Springfield as an arrogant *sense of distinction*. Rebecca and Louise gave me an insight into the phenomenon of 'the Delfin effect', and noted how Greater Springfield's geographic and conceptual isolation from the outside world resulted in a celebration of insularity.

Greater Springfield was a place, according to these informants, that had a clear sense of itself and who its residents could be. But this sense of self was informed heavily by the ideals of the developers and the subsequent ordering and spatialization of the built environment. Along with what I had seen through my own observations, Rebecca noted that, as one example, Greater

Springfield was a very isolating place for teenagers and young adults and went on to suggest that unless you were either a young family or retiree, Greater Springfield couldn't effectively cater to you; it simply wasn't built for groups of people like teenagers. This was a place that, via its physicality and the sorts of actions and behaviours (or, *lifestyle choices*) that were promoted within it, set about identifying a type of individual according to the sort of space it was. This was the cultural logic in action. This logic established who and what the place was and subsequently who and what its people could be.

Part way through my time in Greater Springfield, I thought to myself that alternative visions of Greater Springfield would have had a hard time competing with the Springfield Land Corporation and Delfin visions, if they had indeed existed. The dominance that the Springfield Land Corporation and Delfin exerted as the developers of the space meant that a seemingly monological expression of what the place meant was displayed as *the* expression of Greater Springfield. With this vision of Greater Springfield beamed in idealised gloss from billboards and brochures, and mediated via the sheer scale and physicality of the development's design, it emerged that the modes of living available to residents were largely pre-fabricated according to the lifestyle choices prescribed in the 'vision'. As representatives of the development companies did their best to convince me that there was something to cater to almost everyone in Greater Springfield, it remained that a certain type of person, living a certain type of lifestyle, was the target for this place. The types of community groups, the available social activities, the configuration of public space, the style of housing, the emphasis on affluent consumerism, the shopping centres, the types of sport grounds and more told me that there was a 'typical Greater Springfieldian' envisaged for this place, and if this style of life didn't suit you (like it didn't for Jane, Brett and teenagers), there wasn't going to be much for you.

The People of Greater Springfield

Similarity Attraction Theory: Being an image

What about the people of Greater Springfield—what was their role? It's not enough to suggest, as I alluded above, to say that its residents automatically assumed these images of Greater Springfield life. As DeCerteau (1984) reminds us, we must look beyond the cultural *product* and ask questions about the purposes to which it is applied. For me, the genuinely intriguing thing was how comfortably the imagery of Greater Springfield was absorbed and accepted by the majority of people in Greater Springfield. Most of my informants felt that the way the community had been conceptualised and configured was fantastic—Maree stood as a key example of this, particularly when explaining how safe she felt and how convenient the services were.

But while expressions of difference were voiced by informants like Jane and Brett as two examples, what I couldn't understand is why difference of opinion about Greater Springfield wasn't more widely held. The singular views expressed by the Springfield Land Corporation and Delfin appeared as the only perspectives on what Greater Springfield meant. Where was the deliberate appropriation of these models for personal application? Where was the détournément of the public spaces to represent difference? Where was the challenge to the all-encompassing views of community and lifestyle? Or did everyone (other than Jane and Brett) roughly agree with Maree in thinking that this place was fantastic? There simply wasn't any real sense of challenge to the image[1], and where expression of alternative opinion did surface, such as with Jane's thoughts about the place, they became pathologised to the point that even the person holding those views felt as if they were the problem (as Jane noted, she blamed herself because she wasn't a 'community type of person'). In this instance, it wasn't the way the community was developed that was the problem; it was those people who didn't *fit*. There was nothing in terms of an organised, alternative view of what life in Greater Springfield could be, and where elements of difference did occur, they were pathologised as negative and anti-community.

I argue that the image machine deployed in the development of Greater Springfield affected such a good job that only those people intended for Greater Springfield moved into it. As I noted above, a specific demographic of residents was *intended* for Greater Springfield—namely an affluent middle class. This economic determinant was then compounded with the expressions of style required in the place via distinction embedded in expressions of cultural capital. With the type of person identified and beamed back via billboards and brochures, Greater Springfield became a place of largely homogenous views about lifestyle; in short, it became an enclave of largely similar people.

I argue that a 'similarity-attraction' (Chatman and O'Reilly 2004) process was in operation here. The process of developing Greater Springfield led to the formation of a specific aesthetic that attached to the class/race/gender attributes of the built environment under construction. Via the imagery and themes presented by the billboards, brochures and other artifacts, a clear sense of who the Greater Springfieldian *is* was developed

---

[1] Even that key expression of urban resistance, graffiti, was limited to mostly random tags and base vandalism.

and extended beyond economic-demographic categories alone (that is, beyond the idealised and largely held view that Greater Springfield was a place for affluent middle-class young families and retirees), to also inform the expressions of themes of leisure, lifestyle and affluence that the modes of living available in Greater Springfield afforded. Chatman and O'Reilly note that 'people are attracted to and prefer to spend time with others who hold attitudes that are similar to their own' (2004:193); in Greater Springfield the mechanisms for attracting people to the area, forming the built environment and maintaining a sense of connectedness and community for residents were captured by the logic of affluent middle-class-ness presented via a concern for leisure, belonging, family, consumerism and those other themes displayed on the billboards and brochures of the place. A similarity-attraction process that saw the Greater Springfieldian as the sort of person the billboards depicted, living the sort of life and engaged in the sort of pursuits presented by these artifacts, mediated what the place was and who called it home. This was an educative process, mediated from 10 metres in the air via the fronts of billboards. Residents *learned* about themselves and their community as they encountered these signs *and* each other.

Naturally, the marketers of Greater Springfield knew to market towards key demographics—in this case an affluent market segment. It was against this that ideals of comfortable lifestyle, space and modern conveniences were symbolic reminders of who this group was to be. The attraction of people fitting this identity then went to reinforce this very idea by simply being *who they were*. That is what the development was about. Here was a self-fulfilling logic—a language game of community that residents fell into via a set of discernible identity characteristics that happened to fit what Greater Springfield was intended to be. I can't get past the reference made by Nicole, the development company representative, when I spoke with her early on in this project; she noted that the people featured in the billboards and brochures were indeed Springfield residents (albeit carefully selected ones as Rebecca later told me). Here were residents who became what they saw themselves as being. The reinforcement of the values underpinning these identities manifested as archetypes on towering billboards and ubiquitous community newsletters that fulfilled the logic of Greater Springfield by perpetuating the myth of the Greater Springfieldian; that same person who simultaneously looked on at these billboards at the same time as they appeared in them.

Living Greater Springfield

Apart from what was displayed by the artifacts and people of Greater

Springfield, it was the identity characteristics I didn't see represented that became significant indicators of what Greater Springfield was. Why was it that I didn't see anything other than white faces on the billboards and brochures?[2] Why did an imagined middle-class aesthetic of comfortable affluence pervade these images when the development was set amongst other socially and economically deflated neighbouring suburbs? Why were gender traits only deployed in very stereotypical heterosexualized ways? Where were the teenagers and age groups that weren't associated with young families and retirees? People who occupied identity locations away from those presented in the billboards did exist in Greater Springfield—I had seen them and spoken with them. My informants had also identified diversity in the area; Rebecca had identified a rich diversity of age, ethnicity and sexuality locations in her own street and neighbourhood. The lack of representation of diversity of identities represented by the signs stood as being significant.

As I noted in *Chapter 4*, Greater Springfield was heavily marketed as being the sort of place *you* wanted it to be. But who the '*you*' is—who the subject of this intended lifestyle might be—is left vague until the image of the Greater Springfieldian, built from the amalgam of selected residents and other archetypal signifiers carried by the signs, is deciphered. Other 'types' of people may well have lived in Greater Springfield, and the brochures might have suggested a sort of inclusivity in the development, but in reality, the idea of the Greater Springfieldian was very specific and was mediated very carefully, resulting in an image of the place that neglected the experiences and identity locations of anyone who didn't fit the archetype.

While I'm not suggesting that Greater Springfield needs to be *the* place for 'others', it didn't do much of a job of challenging stereotypes of 'normal' when I was there. And this, in a development whose chairman is an expatriate Malaysian (with a noticeably different accent and skin colour to the dominant ethnic location of the subjects in the artifacts)! Again, this is the operation of the cultural logic of Greater Springfield, where certain values, attributes and characteristics are expressed and maintained via signs, and from which wider paleosymbolic ideals (such as the sorts of lifestyles, leisure pursuits and family structures that might be lived in this place) derive. This isn't a place of choices at all, but a place that maintains a very specific set of identity characteristics for its intended residents. To be in Greater

---

[2] The only non-white faces I noted were those of the jazz musicians in the Brookwater 'Compromise' billboard, as discussed in *Chapter 3*. But again, these musicians, by the logic of the billboard, weren't residents but were the hired entertainment, maintaining the suggestion that Brookwater at least was a 'white' development.

Springfield, according to the signs and experience of it, meant inhabiting a very specific identity location.

Public Pedagogical Interpretations of Urban Spaces: Some Final Thoughts

I started this book by noting the central role signs play in shaping and signifying urban space, with this concern carried into the explorations of Greater Springfield presented in *Chapters 3* and *4*. In terms of what these experiences have taught me about the nature of contemporary urban settings, I found the blatant corporatization of specific ideals—significant community oriented concerns such as *belonging* and more personalised notions such as *happiness* and *fulfilment*—difficult to grapple with. While I've long been interested in the way that public space comes to be used to present the ideas of private concerns, I was amazed at how dominantly signage in public space was deployed in Greater Springfield. Equally amazing were the frequency and 'gloss' of the various newsletters and brochures that were distributed in the place. The marketing machine deployed in Greater Springfield was an effective one, and for me, this was an indication of how processes of 'branding' have become an almost standard element in the construction of things like housing developments. The world is an increasingly marketed and marketable commodity, to the point that even our experiences of those spaces closest in (our homes and those activities that occur within and around them) fall prey to marketing imagery. In Greater Springfield the experience of community was especially open to the spin of idealised representation.

But it was how I gained access to these expressions of Greater Springfield that has held the most significance for me. As an ethnographer, I simply just had to be there to gain a clear insight into what the space meant publicly. It was in the zone of the streetscape that I gathered a rich understanding of collective life that set the context for the bulk of my work. As such the streetscape of Greater Springfield functioned as a transitory location in which I saw the ebb and flow of cultural processes. It was also a space that inculcated me as a flâneur; an observer who looked around as I walked through the street space and took in what Greater Springfield meant.

This was the essence of the streetscape in Greater Springfield. Outside of its basic utilitarian purpose as a part of a transportation network, it also operated as a major location of cultural production. The street, that place from which I looked at Greater Springfield and situated my discussions with its residents, was a proximal 'outside' zone that I initially (at the commencement of this project) didn't fully appreciate. The street is the teacher we don't even realise is there; sending out imagery and signage at every turn, requiring mediated behaviours as we negotiate the people and places it leads to, and drawing on accumulated knowledge (our 'street smarts') to safely arrive at the destinations we set out for. The everyday-ness of the street masks its influence; the mundanity of the street as a product of urbanized landscapes sees us encountering these spaces regularly but unquestioningly. It is the influence these spaces exert that matters; the mediations the street exercise offer an insight into the way we live as 'rapidly privatized and individualised' (Bauman 2001:15) members of the contemporary, globalized world.

We become unwitting flâneurs in these information-rich streetscapes. For the flâneur, that street walker and social critic originally of *fin de siecle* Paris, the street offered a key location to watch and be consumed by the play of the social:

> The flâneur lives his life as a succession of absolute beginnings. From the past, there is an easy exit; the present is just a gateway; the future is not yet, and what is not yet cannot bind. (Bauman 1994:139)

It is the flâneur that:

> ...is like a detective seeking clues who reads people's characters not only from the physiognomy of their faces but via a social physiognomy of the street. (Shields 1994:63)

From his (as the original flâneur was only ever a man) reading of the street—from this detective-like gathering of information on the street—the flâneur operates as a fixed point on the temporal continuum of the street. It is he who stops to exert his reading, his observation of the streetscape in order to fix it in a point in time and space. But to say that the flâneur is dead, gone with the arcades of 1890s Paris, denies that we are all, as street-users, implicated in a flânerie of necessity in this period of late capitalism. We find ourselves exposed to a range of message systems in the streetscape—information networks that represent the global village in our very own local thoroughfares. It is the street that exposes us, in our corner of the world to the multiple discourses of the urban environment. The street is an open location away from our comfort points in the home, shopping mall or school. A space that is inhabited, common, invested with multiple meanings and ownerships simultaneously. It is a site for the operation of public pedagogies.

As such, we must be critical in our contemporary flâneurist pursuits. The street isn't a neutral space, but one contested with claims and power plays. As with Greater Springfield, where significant agency to determine what the space meant was held by the developers' of the place, the street is a location of specific interests and appropriations; this is the nature of our neo-liberal, globalized and late-capitalist world, in which informal, public pedagogical activity occurs increasingly in public spaces. As Giroux (2004) reminds us, 'profound transformations have taken place in the public space' (498), with the street functioning as both active host of artifacts of public pedagogical production (such as the roadside billboard) and as a pedagogical force of its own contextualization. As urban flâneurs we negotiate our streetscapes whilst being bombarded with information flows, each drawing their own discursive formations and identity-forming practices.

It is this that incorporates us as flâneurs. We absorb the flows and constructions of the street and its streetscape and interact as individuals contextualized by the urban environment. We read our way through our urban habitus with the street guiding our path to those key points of destination. We perform meaning-construction acts as we pass through and as it responds to us, sending us images and representations from our global world. The street as both a physical entity and imagined space is implicit in the construction of meaning via this public pedagogical capacity. The street warrants more serious attention from us; as a location of the production of culture and a location in which discursive formations find meaning, we as unwitting flâneurs should enter it with a critical capacity to determine and deconstruct the messages it beams to us. That, for me, has been the lesson of my time in Greater Springfield; the street is no neutral place. As a key location within the urban environs we inhabit, the street is that intermediary from which we learn and find-out about our selves. But *who* it is that arbitrates what we see in this ever-corporatized public space, and *how* it is we come to consume these images, that is the point of significance.

References

Addington, P. 2002. *Unreal City*. Available from www.bbc.co.uk/dna/filmnetwork/A4185344.

Anderson, B. 1983. *Imagined Communities: Reflections on the Origin and Spread of Nationalism*. New York: Cornell University Press.

Appardurai, A. 1996. *Modernity at Large: Cultural Dimensions of Globalisation*. Minneapolis: University of Minnesota Press.

Australian Unity. 2007. *Wellbeing Index: Report 12.1 Special Report on City and Country Living*. Available from www.australianunity.com.au/info/wellbeing/default.asp.

Barthes, R. 1972. *Mythologies*. New York: Hill and Wang.

Bartlett, A. 2006. *A Crisis in Housing Affordability*. Available from http://www.onlineopinion.com.au/view.asp?article=4834.

Baudrillard, J. 1994. *Simulacra and Simulation*. Ann Arbour: University of Michigan Press.

Bauman, Z. 1994. "Desert Spectacular". Pp. 138–157 in K. Tester, ed., *The Flâneur*. London: Routledge.

———. 2001. *Community: Seeking Safety in an Insecure World*. Cambridge: Polity.

———. 2007. *Liquid Times: Living in an Age of Uncertainty*. Cambridge: Polity.

Bayet, A. 1997. "Un-Civil Society: The Politics of the 'Informal People'". *Third World Quarterly* 18:53–72.

Borer, M. I. 2006. "The Location of Culture: The Urban Culturalist Perspective". *City & Community* 5:173–197.

Bourdieu, P. 1987. *Distinction: A Social Critique of the Judgement of Taste*. Cambridge: Harvard University Press.

Bridge, G. 2005. *Reason in the City of Difference: Pragmatism, Communicative Action and Contemporary Urbanism*. New York: Routledge.

Brower, S. 1996. *Good Neighbourhoods: A Study of In-Town and Suburban Residential Environments*. Westport: Praeger.

Caldeira, T.P.R. 2005. "Fortified Enclaves: The New Urban Segregation". Pp. 83–110 in S.M. Low, ed., *Theorizing the City: The New Urban Anthropology Reader*. New Brunswick: Rutgers University Press.

———. 1999. *City of Walls: Crime, Segregation and Citizenship in Sao Paulo*. Berkeley, University of California Press.

Chatman, J. and O'Reilly, C. 2004. "Asymmetric Reactions to Work Group Sex Diversity Among Men and Women", *Academy of Management Journal*, 47:193–208.

Clark, D. 2003. *Urban World/Global City*. New York: Routledge.

Cochrane, P. 2007. "Springfield Lakes the Place to Be". *Urban Development Review* (April).

Cohen, A.P. 2004. *The Symbolic Construction of Community*. London: Routledge.

Colombijn, F., and Erdentug, A. 2002. *Urban Ethnic Encounters: The Spatial Consequences*. London: Routledge.

Connell, R. 2007. *Southern Theory: The Global Dynamics of Knowledge in Social Science*. St. Leonards: Allen and Unwin.

Crook, A. 2005. "Who Says We're All Miserable?" *Manchester Evening News* (13th March).

Cummins, R.A., Davern, M., Okerstrom, E., Lo, S.K., and Eckersley, R. 2005. *Australian Unity Wellbeing Index: Report 12.1 Special Report on City and Country Living*. Available from www.australianunity.com.au/info/wellbeing/default.asp.

David, E. 2007. "Signs of Resistance: Marking Renewed Public Space through a Renewed Cultural Activism". Pp. 225–253 in G.C. Stanczak, ed., *Visual Research Methods: Image, Society, and Representation*. Thousand Oaks: SAGE.

Davis, M. 2000. *Magical Urbanism: Latinos Reinvent the U.S. Big City*. New York: Verso.

———. 2000. *Ecology of Fear: Los Angeles and the Imagination of Disaster*. New York: Vintage.

DeCerteau, M. 1998. *The Practice of Everyday Life*. Berkeley: University of California Press.

Demerath, L., and Levinger, D. 2003. "The Social Qualities of Being on Foot: A Theoretical Analysis of Pedestrian Activity, Community and Culture". *City & Community* 2: 217–237.

Denzin, N.K., and Lincoln, Y.S., eds. 2005. *The SAGE Handbook of Qualitative Research, 3rd ed*. Thousand Oaks: SAGE.

Duncanson, N. 2006. "Grin-It City". *Daily Record* (28th April).

Engels, F. 2009. *The Condition of the Working Class in England*. Oxford: OUP.

Flanagan, W. 2001. *Urban Sociology: Images and Structure, 4th ed*. New York: Allyn & Bacon.

Frazier, E.F. 1932. *The Negro Family in Chicago*. Chicago: University of Chicago Press.

Frers, L., and Meier, L. 2007. *Encountering Urban Places: Visual and Material Performances in the City*. Aldershot: Ashgate.

Geertz, C. 1973. "Thick Description: Toward an Interpretive Theory of Culture". Pp. 3–30 in *The Interpretation of Cultures: Selected Essays*. New York: Basic Books.

Giroux, H.A. 2001. *The Mouse That Roared: Disney and the End of Innocence*. Lanham: Rowman and Littlefield.

———. 2004. "Public Pedagogy and the Politics of Neo-Liberalism: Making the Political More Pedagogical". *Policy Futures in Education* 2:494–503.

Glasser, B.G., and Shapiro, J.M. 2003. "Urban Growth in the 1990's: Is City Living Black?" *Journal of Regional Science* 43:139–165.

Gottdiener, M., and Hutchison, R. 2006. *The New Urban Sociology, 3rd ed*. Cambridge: Westview Press.

Graham, K.A.H., and Peters, E.J. 2002. *Aboriginal Community and Urban Sustainability: Discussion Paper F/27*. Ottawa: Canadian Policy Research Network.

Grange, J. 1999. *The City: An Urban Cosmology*. New York: State University of New York Press.

Hall, T., and Miles, M. 2003. *Urban Futures: Critical Commentaries on Shaping the City*. New York: Routledge.

Hamel, P., Lustiger-Thaler, H., and Mayer, M. 2000. *Urban Movements in a Globalizing World*. London: Routledge.

Harper, D. 1990. "The Visual Ethnographic Narrative". *Visual Anthropology* 1:1–19.

———. 2006. "The Visual Ethnographic Narrative". Pp. 1121–1145 in P. Hamilton, ed., *Visual Research Methods Volume 3*. Thousand Oaks: SAGE.

Harvey, D. 1990. *The Condition of Postmodernity: An Enquiry into the Origins of Cultural Change*. Oxford: Blackwell.

Hayner, N. 1936. *Hotel Life*. Chapel Hill: University of North Carolina Press.

Hebdidge, D. 1988. *Hiding in the Light: On Images and Things*. London: Comedia.

Hickey, A., and Austin, J. 2006. *(Re)Presenting Education: Students, Teachers, Schools and the Public Imagination*. Frenchs Forest: Pearson.

Holston, J. 1999. *Cities and Citizenship*. Durham: Duke University Press.

Hosagrahar, J. 2005. *Indigenous Modernities: Negotiating Architecture and Urbanism*. New York: Routledge.

Jameson, F. 1991. *Postmodernism: Or, The Cultural Logic of Late Capitalism*. Durham: Duke.

Karp, D.A., Stone, G.P., and Yoels, W.C. 1991. *Being Urban: A Sociology of City Life*, 2nd ed. Westport: Greenwood.

Kincheloe, J. 2002. *The Sign of the Burger: McDonalds and the Culture of Power*. Philadelphia: Temple University Press.

Lebo, L. 2007. "City Life Focus of Group's Fair". *Daily Record* (13th January).

Lefebvre, H. 1991. *The Production of Space*. London: Blackwell.

Light, I. 1983. *Cities in World Perspective*. New York: Macmillan.

Malpas, S. 2001. *Postmodernism*. Oxford: OUP.

MacCannell, D. 1999. *The Tourist: A New Theory of the Leisure Class*. Berkeley: University of California Press.

McMillan, D., and Chavis, D.M. 1986. "Sense of Community: A Definition and Theory". *Journal of Community Psychology* 14:6–23.

Merry, S.E. 1981. *Urban Danger: Life in a Neighbourhood of Strangers*. Philadelphia: Temple University Press.

Minca, C., ed. 2001. *Postmodern Geography: Theory and Practice*. Malden: Blackwell.

Mommaas, H. 2004. "Cultural Clusters and the Post-Industrial City: Towards the Remapping of Urban Cultural Policy". *Urban Studies* 41:507–532.

O'Connor, R.A. 1995. "Indigenous Urbanism: Class, City and Society in Southeast Asia". *Journal of Asian Studies* 26:30–45.

Park, R. 1927. Unpublished Quote Recorded by Howard Becker.

———. 1925/1967. "The City: Suggestions for the Investigation of Human Behaviour in the Urban Environment," in R.Park, E.W. Burgess, and R.D. McKenzie, eds., *The City*. Chicago: University of Chicago Press.

Parker, S. 2004. *Urban Theory and the Urban Experience*. London: Routledge.

Peters, E.J. 1998. "Subversive Spaces: First Nations Women and the City". *Society and Space* 16:665–685.

———. 2001. "Developing Federal Policy for First Nations People in Urban Areas 1945–1975". *The Canadian Journal of Native Studies* 10:57–96.

Popcorn, F. 1992. *The Popcorn Report*. New York: Collins.

Rodriguez, J.A. 1999. *City against Suburb: The Culture Wars in an American Metropolis*. Westport: Praeger.

Roy, A., and Al Sayyad, N. 2004. *Urban Informality: Transnational Perspectives from the Middle East, Latin America and South Asia*. Oxford: Lexington Books.

Saukko, P. 2005. "Methodologies for Cultural Studies: An Integrative Approach". Pp. 343–356 in N.K. Denzin and Y.S. Lincoln, eds., *The SAGE Handbook of Qualitative Research*, 3rd ed. Thousand Oaks: SAGE.

Schutzman, M. 1999. *The Real Thing: Performance, Hysteria and Advertising*. Middletown: Wesleyan University Press.

Sennett, R. 1996. *The Uses of Disorder: Personal Identity and City Life*. London: Faber and Faber.

Shields, R. 1994. "Fancy Footwork: Walter Benjamin's Notes on Flânerie". Pp. 61–80 in K. Tester, ed., *The Flâneur*. London: Routledge.

Silberberg, R. 2007. *Housing Affordability Crisis.* Available from http://www.abc.net.au/news/stories/2007/06/01/1939416.htm.

Simmel, G. 1950. "The Stranger". Pp. 402–408 in K. Wolff, ed., *The Sociology of Georg Simmel.* New York: Free Press.

———. 1997a. "The Metropolis and Mental Life" Pp. 174–185 in D. Frisby and M. Featherstone, eds., *Simmel on Culture,* London: SAGE.

———. 1997b. "The Sociology of Space" Pp. 137–169 in D. Frisby and M. Featherstone, eds. *Simmel on Culture.* London: SAGE.

Soja, E. 2000. "Exploring the Postmetropolis". Pp. 37–56 in C. Minca, ed., *Postmodern Geography: Theory and Practice.* Malden: Blackwell.

Spradley, J.P. 1979. *The Ethnographic Interview.* New York: Holt, Reinhart and Winston.

Stencil Revolution. 2008. Available from http://www.stencilrevolution.com/.

Tajbakhsh, K. 2001. *The Promise of the City: Space, Identity and Politics in Contemporary Social Thought.* Berkeley: University of California Press.

Thrasher, F. 1927. *The Gang: A Study of 1.313 Gangs in Chicago.* Chicago: University of Chicago Press.

Timms, E., and Kelly, D., eds. 1985. *Unreal City: Urban Experience in Modern European Literature and Art.* New York: St. Martin's Press.

Tranberg Hansen, K., and Vaa, M., eds. 2004. *Reconsidering Informality: Perspectives from Urban Africa.* Durban: Nordic Africa Institute.

United Nations. 2009. *World Urbanisation Prospects, 2009 Revision.* New York: United Nations Department of Economic and Social Affairs.

Walker, J. 2006. P. 21. in *Sunday Mail Q Weekend* supplement (7th–8th October).

Williams, R. 1989. "Culture Is Ordinary". Pp. 3–14 in *Resources of Hope: Culture, Democracy and Socialism.* London: Verso.

Willis, P. 1977. *Learning to Labour: How Working Class Kids Get Working Class Jobs.* Surrey: Ashgate.

Wirth, L. 1928. *The Ghetto.* Chicago: University of Chicago Press.

Wohl, R., and Strauss, A. 1958. "Symbolic Representation in the Urban Milieu". *American Journal of Sociology* 63:523–532.

Zorbaugh, H. 1929. *The Gold Coast and the Slum: A Sociological Study of Chicago's Near North Side.* Chicago: University of Chicago Press.

Index

About the Author

Andrew T. Hickey is Senior Lecturer in Cultural Studies and Social Theory at the University of Southern Queensland, Australia. In conjunction with his research on public pedagogies and urban space, Andrew has led numerous projects exploring identity, community and race politics and has developed approaches in ethnographic and autoethnographic field practice. He is the author of *(Re)Presenting Education: Students, Teachers, Schools and the Public Imagination* (with Jon Austin), a sociology of schooling and popular cultural representations of education. Andrew lives with his partner and two boys.

minding the media

CRITICAL ISSUES
FOR LEARNING AND TEACHING

Shirley R. Steinberg & Pepi Leistyna
General Editors

Minding the Media is a book series specifically designed to address the needs of students and teachers in watching, comprehending, and using media. Books in the series use a wide range of educational settings to raise consciousness about media relations and realities and promote critical, creative alternatives to contemporary mainstream practices. *Minding the Media* seeks theoretical, technical, and practitioner perspectives as they relate to critical pedagogy and public education. Authors are invited to contribute volumes of up to 85,000 words to this series. Possible areas of interest as they connect to learning and teaching include:

- critical media literacy
- popular culture
- video games
- animation
- music
- media activism
- democratizing information systems
- using alternative media
- using the Web/internet
- interactive technologies
- blogs
- multi-media in the classroom
- media representations of race, class, gender, sexuality, disability, etc.

- media/communications studies methodologies
- semiotics
- watchdog journalism/investigative journalism
- visual culture: theater, art, photography
- radio, TV, newspapers, zines, film, documentary film, comic books
- public relations
- globalization and the media
- consumption/consumer culture
- advertising
- censorship
- audience reception

For additional information about this series or for the submission of manuscripts, please contact:

Shirley R. Steinberg and Pepi Leistyna,
msgramsci@aol.com | Pepi.Leistyna@umb.edu

To order other books in this series, please contact our Customer Service Department:

(800) 770-LANG (within the U.S.)
(212) 647-7706 (outside the U.S.)
(212) 647-7707 FAX

Or browse online by series:

www.peterlang.com

www.ingramcontent.com/pod-product-compliance
Lightning Source LLC
Chambersburg PA
CBHW050611280326
41932CB00016B/2999